The Peter Potts
Book of World Records

CLIFFORD B. HICKS

The
PETER POTTS
Book of World Records

☆

A true account of the astounding
feats of Peter Potts and Joey Gootz,
as witnessed and sworn to by me,

Illustrated by Kathleen Collins Howell

Henry Holt and Company ★ New York

Published by Henry Holt and Company, Inc.,
521 Fifth Avenue, New York, New York 10175.
Published in Canada by Fitzhenry & Whiteside Limited,
195 Allstate Parkway, Markham, Ontario L3R 4T8.

Library of Congress Cataloging-in-Publication Data
Hicks, Clifford B.
The Peter Potts book of world records.
Summary: Although he is angry and confused because
of the impending arrival of his older sister's baby
in a family he thinks is already perfect, twelve-
year-old Pete finds a welcome distraction in his best
friend's disastrous attempts to set several new
world records.
[1. World records—Fiction.   2. Babies—Fiction]
I. Howell, Kathleen Collins, ill.   II. Title.
PZ7.H5316Pf   1987   [Fic]   87-19795

ISBN: 0-8050-0409-2

First Edition

Designer: Victoria Hartman
Printed in the United States of America
10 9 8 7 6 5 4 3 2 1

ISBN 0-8050-0409-2

With much love
for the real Angela Sue

Contents

The Peter Potts
Book of World Records

The World's Largest Cotton Candy Machine

Joey Gootz is my best friend.

Joey Gootz is also the world's weirdest kid. That's just one of the world's records Joey holds, even though he doesn't *try* to be the world's weirdest kid.

I don't know how Joey got hooked on world's records. He's been that way as long as I can remember. He just automatically thinks in terms of the biggest in the world, or the smallest, or the highest, or the smartest. I think he was born that way.

Like this morning. We were in the middle of a mudball fight along the banks of Avery Creek when Joey hollered, "The heaviest woman who ever lived was Mrs. Percy Washington, who weighed 880 pounds." While I was trying to digest that bit of information I lowered the garbage-can lid I carried as a shield, and Joey got me in the Adam's apple. It hurt like fury.

Other kids talk about sports, but Joey talks about

sports *records.* Yesterday we were catching crickets down in Goose Hollow when he said, "Clarence Francis of Rio Grande College scored the most points ever in a college basketball game."

"How many?"

"On February 2, 1954, he scored 113 points in a game against Hillsdale College."

As soon as I get home, after I've been with Joey, I write down all the things he's said that I can remember. Like:

"The smallest fish ever caught in a fishing contest was a smelt that weighed one-sixteenth of an ounce."

"William Fuqua of Fort Worth, Texas, stayed perfectly motionless in a department store window for 4½ hours to set a new world's record."

"Charles Osborne started hiccuping in 1922, and is still going strong. He can't keep his false teeth in his mouth."

Joey gets most of these gems from a shelf of world's record books right above his bed. He'd rather read them than eat blueberry pie.

Joey is just five days younger than I am. Last May, for five days, I was twelve and Joey was still eleven. It happens that way every year, and every year I rub it in.

We both live in Fairfield, which I know for a fact is the world's greatest little town to grow up in.

Actually, Joey lives in town, but I live with Pop on a farm out on the edge of Fairfield. Pop is not really my father. He's my grandfather, but everybody in town calls him Pop, so I do, too.

My sister Betts and I came to live with Pop when our parents were killed in an automobile accident eight years ago. Betts is eight years older than I am. After we came to live with Pop, she became my half-mother, half-sister, and half-special-friend, if you can have one-and-a-half halves.

I have only a few memories of my real mother. She sits in front of a mirror, combing her long hair. She hangs onto the mast of a sailboat, looking up at the sky. Once in a while she kneels down in a bed of orange flowers.

Funny, but I never see her face. In these memories, I *know* it's my mother, but there's only a fuzzy gold area where her face is supposed to be.

So Betts has taken over, at least sometimes, the role of my mother. Like when she gave me holy what-for when she caught me trying to buy a child's ticket at the movie, two days after my twelfth birthday.

I get *feelings* about Betts I can't explain. When she's pulling a pan of molasses cookies from the oven, she puckers up her mouth just like my real mother used to do. Don't ask me how I know this. If I can't remember my mother's face, how can I tell when Betts looks just like her, for a moment?

That's why I felt so bad when Betts fell in love with Mike Summers. I suddenly felt left out of her life. I felt alone.

Don't get me wrong. Mike is a nice guy. I knew him before Betts fell in love with him. At any given moment he can tell you where there's a fox den, how to take care of a pheasant with a broken wing, where to look in the lake for bluegill nests.

But when Betts told me that she and Mike were going to get married, I suddenly hated him. I felt like he had stolen her from me.

For a while, after they were married, things worked out fine, just like she said they would. In Pop's old farmhouse there's a big bedroom downstairs and three more bedrooms upstairs. After their honeymoon, Betts and Mike took over the big room downstairs. Betts was still around all the time to make molasses cookies, mainly for me, and turnip stew, mainly for Pop. She still shot baskets with me, and helped me with my homework.

Mike eased into the family, too. He taught me how to catch bass on a plug instead of a worm, and follow a muskrat's trail. He helped me defuse a baby skunk we found in one of Billy Paynter's muskrat traps. We named the skunk Little Stinker, and he was the smartest pet I ever had. Six months ago a car ran over him. I cried, and Betts did, too.

Anyway, the marriage turned out fine. Lots of times when things look their super worst, they eventually turn out to be their super best. You might want to remember that.

I'll never forget the morning Betts told me she was

going to have a baby. I almost flipped. Talk about excitement. I'd probably be the only uncle in Warren G. Harding School!

But a little later, things started to change. Betts said she couldn't shoot baskets with me anymore—the doctor wouldn't let her. She and Mike whispered to each other a lot, as though they were keeping secrets from me. I began to feel like Moose Sanders.

When Moose's mother had a baby brother—I mean when Moose got a baby brother because his mother had a baby—it changed everything for Moose. His mother and father were so busy taking care of the baby that they didn't pay much attention to Moose. Diapers became more important than the fact that Moose finally made the school baseball team.

Moose told me that one day, when he was pretending to hug the baby, he found himself hugging it a little too tightly. That really scared him, to a point where he wouldn't pick up the baby for weeks.

Whenever Betts carried on about *her* baby, I began feeling like Moose.

"Oh, Pete, I'm so happy! My own baby to love, and take care of, and dress, and show off to everybody." We were washing the dishes. She glanced at me, and must have seen a strange look on my face because she corrected herself. "*Our* baby, Pete."

"You mean *Mike's* baby," I said in a low voice. "Not mine."

"Of course. But *your* baby, too, Pete. Just wait until

he can walk, and talk. You can take him camping at West Bluffs, and teach him to throw a baseball, and show him where to find night crawlers."

I got up and headed for the back door. "How do you know it's going to be a boy?"

"It's got to be." She was talking to my back, and there was a note of worry in her voice. "I've already made up my mind. It's got to be a boy, Pete, so he can grow up to be just like you. We haven't even discussed a name for a girl."

"Probably be a girl!" I shouted back at her. "Anyway, I don't care!"

I slammed the screen door.

★ ★ ★

Well, I can't complain. At least not much. I've still got Joey as a best friend to grow up with. Joey and his world's records.

It was late last spring, just after we'd spent a day at the American Legion carnival, that Joey came up with his brainstorm. We weren't just going to *talk about* world's records; we were going to *set them ourselves*!

We were horsing around down in his dad's basement workshop. Suddenly Joey's eyes glazed over. He ran his fingers like a comb through his kinky red hair.

"The world's largest cotton candy machine!" he said.

"Who built it?" I asked.

"We did. Today."

Joey doesn't ordinarily talk very much except when he's quoting world's records. Just a few words are a long sentence to Joey. You learn to pay attention to each of those words. I've found that people who don't say much say it loudest. You might want to remember that.

"How are we going to build a giant cotton candy machine?" I asked.

"All we need is a big rotating pan, and some heat. World's largest cotton candy machine."

"What'll we use for a pan?"

Joey thought for a moment. "Out in the garage. Above the car."

I followed him outside. He unfolded a stepladder in the garage, and climbed to the top. Some old sheets of plywood had been nailed across the garage bracing, forming a big shelf. Joey pulled out a kids' plastic wading pool. He handed it down to me. It was covered with dust and grime.

Back in the basement, Joey got an electric motor off a shelf. There was a big pulley on the shaft. "Three horsepower," he said proudly. "Took it off Mrs. Grimsby's old washer."

I watched while he built the cotton candy machine, helping when he told me what to do. He nailed to-gether some two-by-four scraps until he had a kind of platform in the middle of the basement floor. I helped him screw the electric motor to the platform. We fastened it on its side, so the pulley was on top. The pulley had three holes in it.

Joey had me hold the wading pool while he estimated where the center was. He drilled three holes through the plastic, and then bolted the wading pool to the pulley.

The whole contraption looked a little goofy crouching there in the middle of the shop floor. He hadn't done a very good job of eyeballing the center of the wading pool, but I didn't say anything.

He stared at the machine for a minute. Then he said, "Heat."

"Heat," I repeated. "What for?"

"Got to heat up the sugar. Then it'll melt and spin out into cotton candy."

He went upstairs. When he came back he was carrying a portable electric heater, a ten-pound bag of sugar, and a bottle of red food coloring. He placed them on the workbench, and plugged in the electric heater. Its built-in fan made a whirring noise.

Joey handed the heater to me. "Aim it at the middle of the wading pool," he instructed.

I leaned over the pool and focused the heater.

Joey opened the bag of sugar and dumped all ten pounds into the middle of the pool. I waggled the heater at it. Joey dribbled the bottle of food coloring over the sugar.

By now the heater was getting warm in my hands. "Hurry up!" I said.

Joey picked up the electric cord from the motor, and walked over to a wall outlet. He turned around and stared at the machine. I did, too. I didn't know what to expect. In the middle of the huge pan was an uneven mound of sugar, crisscrossed with a crazy quilt of red lines. The heater was shaking in my hands just above the mound.

"Looks great," Joey said calmly. "World's Largest Cotton Candy Machine. New record."

He plugged in the motor.

The wading pool moved very slowly, slewing around in a big circle. As it gained speed it started moaning. It really was weird.

The mound of red sugar began to disappear before my eyes. At first I thought the heater in my hands was melting it. Then I noticed that the sugar was being slung out toward the rim of the revolving wading pool.

The heater had grown so hot it was burning my hands. I couldn't stand it any longer. I flipped the switch on the heater, jumped backward, and dropped the heater on the floor.

It's a good thing I did.

By now the pool was spinning wildly, and the moan had risen to a throbbing scream. At that point it started slinging melted red sugar all over the basement. It didn't sling it in a nice even coat either. The pool was off center, so it slung out the sugar in big globs. One hit me in the stomach, and moved me three feet to the rear.

I glanced over at Joey just in time to see a blob hit him in the face. It was a strange color—kind of a dirty plum. Even in all the excitement, I wondered why. Then I remembered that we hadn't cleaned the dirt out of the wading pool.

"Unplug it!" I shouted over the shriek of the World's Largest Cotton Candy Machine.

Joey couldn't find the plug. He couldn't find it because he couldn't see. He staggered across the room trying to rub the dirty red sugar out of his eyes.

I dodged past him and reached for the plug.

Just then there was a crack like a cannon going off. The wading pool tore loose and sailed right past Joey's head. It hit the basement wall and was spinning so hard it ran right on around the room.

I unplugged the motor.

Sudden silence.

I looked around the basement. Big globs of dirty-red sugar speckled the walls and ceiling. I reached out and scooped one off with my fingers. It was warm and sticky. Tasted good, but not much like cotton candy.

Joey's face looked like a handful of rotten plums. The only place you could see his skin was two big trickles below his eyes, where tears had washed down through the sugar.

I felt like heading out of there and swimming toward China.

The silence was broken by a snicker. I looked over at Joey. A big smile cracked through his purple face. The snicker turned into a giggle, then a laugh.

Joey reached over and pounded me on the back. I started laughing, too. We sat down on the floor and laughed ourselves silly.

Later, Joey's parents talked to Pop about the mess in the basement. Of course I had to help clean it up.

We did the best we could. Then we were sentenced to a whole week without seeing each other. On the fifth day, the Aldrich twins smuggled me a note.

"Ants all over the basement" was all it said.

THE WORLD'S LARGEST
COTTON CANDY MACHINE.

The huge contraption was built by Joey Gootz and Peter Potts in the basement of Joey's home at 247 Hickory Lane in Fairfield on May 18, and put into operation at 3:48 that date. The results were spectacular, and eventually the machine converted itself into the World's First Motorized Cotton—Candy Ant Farm. I witnessed the event and swear that to the best of my knowledge we set a new world's record.

Peter Potts

☆ 2 ☆

The World's Largest Box Kite

Joey Gootz's brain must have a lot of weird alleyways, and nerve splices, and hidden pockets, and dead ends. I never can tell how his mind moves along from one thought to another. Joey can be very busy *doing* something, and yet be *thinking* about something entirely different.

That's what happened last June. Joey and I were celebrating the first day of summer vacation by starting to build our long-planned dam across Coon Dog Creek. The dam would provide us with our own private swimming pool.

We'd tossed three logs into the muddy creek as a base for the dam, and then searched along the creek banks for rocks to fill in the cracks between the logs. Joey found a big boulder and gave it a heave. At the same time, he shouted, "The World's Largest Box Kite!"

The boulder struck the mud right in front of me. I

jumped back, but still got splatted all over. "Whose?" I said, wiping mud out of my eyes.

"Ours. We'll set a new record."

Every summer vacation Joey and I build a kite, just as regular as crawdads appear in Coon Dog Creek come early June. We've become famous among the kids in Fairfield for our kites.

"Sounds great to me," I said. I was soaking wet, and tired of working on the dam. "Let's go build it." Joey is great on ideas, but sometimes he's not so hot at carrying them out.

On the way home, Joey made a little sideways skip every three or four steps. He was excited. "What'll we make the box kite out of?" he asked. I knew then that he'd turned control of the project over to me.

"We'll start with poles about twelve feet long." The kite was already beginning to take shape in my mind. "We'll nail them into a framework, and cover it with cloth."

"Man! That's BIG! Twelve feet high!" He whistled. "Need help flying it. Maybe the Aldrich twins?"

I instantly agreed. The Aldrich twins, Grady and Brady, are big for their age, and as strong as two identical bulls.

"Hey!" I said. "We've got to get Timmy Belasco out there for our test flight, too." Timmy wouldn't be of any help in launching the kite, but he *belonged* there with us.

Maybe, sometime during your life, you've had a

special feeling about another kid who isn't anywhere near your age. That's how Joey and I feel about little Timmy Belasco.

Timmy lives next door to Joey. He's six years old. We adopted him when he came about to our kneecaps. Don't ask me why. Over the years Joey and I have taught him to ride a two-wheeler, and catch bluegills, and how to make a slingshot. We call him "Kiddo." He follows us wherever we go around town, except that he can't keep up anymore.

About a year ago, Timmy began losing weight and looked kind of sickly. Gradually he got weaker. Now he can't keep up with us or the other kids, and lots of times his folks push him around in a wheelchair. They told Joey and me that there's something wrong with Kiddo's kidneys, and the doctor is talking about a kidney transplant.

Yes, Timmy had to be there when we launched the World's Biggest Box Kite.

When we got to my house, we headed out to the toolshed. Years ago, Pop used the shed to repair his farm machinery. Now he uses it as a workshop for his hobbies. He gave up farming a few years ago, and now does odd jobs around Fairfield, except when he's hobbying.

If Pop doesn't have a hobby he's grindy as a lonesome bull. Last week he finally gave up trying to perfect his perpetual motion machine, and didn't speak to the rest of us for three days. Then he got the notion to invent a burglar alarm—one that sprays fluorescent paint all over the intruder so you can identify him later. Right away he returned to our lovable old Pop.

We thought we might find some lumber for the box kite in Pop's toolshed, but there wasn't anything there. Pop's perpetual motion machine was standing in one corner. I gave it a spin. It clanked away for about thirty seconds, then ground to a stop.

Joey was leaning against one of the two-by-two studs that held up the old building. Suddenly he patted the stud. "Don't need all of these," he said.

"We don't?"

"Not *we*. The building. Half as many studs would hold up this toolshed. Anyway, we'll only take four. Nail them back up later."

I got his drift right away. If you get really excited about a goal in life, nothing can stand in your way. You can overcome any obstacle. That's a good thought for the day. It explains everything from a mosquito bite to the Egyptian pyramids.

I picked up a crowbar from Pop's bench, and Joey grabbed a hammer. The nails were so rusty it was hard work, but we finally pried loose every other two-by-two until we had four boards about twelve feet long.

Some of the siding came loose with one of the studs, leaving a hole in the wall. Right beside the hole was a 1954 calendar. I took it down and nailed it over the hole, figuring that if Pop hadn't looked at the calendar in all those years he wouldn't notice I'd moved it.

Pop has an old do-it-yourself encyclopedia. In volume 10 (KA–LO) we found plans for a box kite two feet high. Ours was going to be twelve feet high, so we just multiplied all the dimensions by six.

After we drew up some rough plans, Joey headed for home. I went into the house to make some phone calls to recruit other kids. Betts was painting the kitchen cabinets. Light blue. Yuk.

"Hi, Pete," she said, flashing me a smile.

"What're you doing?" I asked, as if I didn't know.

"Painting the kitchen cabinets." Dumb answer.

"Why?"

"Just brightening up the place for the baby."

The baby. The *baby*.

I'll bet she never even *thought* of painting the kitchen cabinets for *me*.

I lifted the lid on the cookie jar. It was empty.

I started through the door without saying a word. I didn't even look at her.

"Wait, Pete. I'm sorry. I'd planned to bake molasses cookies this afternoon, but I got carried away with this paint job. Now there's not enough time before dinner."

"Not enough time," I said. "Not enough time for *me*. Seems like that's been happening a lot lately, and the baby isn't even here yet."

It was a mean thing to say. Ordinarily I wouldn't be mean to Betts for the world. I glanced at her. There was a hurt look in her eyes.

"I'm sorry, Pete." Her voice was so soft I hardly heard it.

I slammed out of the kitchen, and made my phone calls. First, because it was the most important, I made arrangements for Timmy Belasco to see the kite-launch the next morning. His voice was weak, but he sounded excited.

"Take it easy, Kiddo," I said. "Just thought you might help Joey and me fly a kite." I didn't tell him how big that kite would be.

Then I called the Aldrich twins and about a dozen other kids. They all agreed to help.

So did Angela Hibbs and Sue Long. They're the two best girls in the business of being girls.

★   ★   ★

Saturday turned out to be a gusty early summer day, with big gray clouds chasing each other across the sky. Most of the time you couldn't see the sun. We would have preferred a strong, steady wind with no gusts, but over the phone Joey and I decided to build our kite and give it a test flight despite the weather.

About nine o'clock Joey came walking up our drive pulling Timmy Belasco in a coaster wagon. Lately, it seemed to me, Timmy's eyes had been kind of dull, but this morning they were shining like stars. He looked mighty thin though.

"Hi, Kiddo," I called from the front door. "You had any breakfast?"

"Hey, Pete!" he called, his smile as big as his face. "Where's the kite? Let's go!"

I brought out some raisins, but Timmy was too excited to eat them so Joey and I did.

About five minutes later the Aldrich twins showed up to help us haul the boards and tools.

Highway 12 runs right past our house, and across the highway is Oostermeyer's pasture. It's mostly level, and a good place to fly a kite. When we crossed the highway, we found ten or twelve other kids waiting for us. Noah Oostermeyer's big black bull watched us from behind the fence next door.

Each of the kids had brought along something for the kite. Willie Duff supplied a long piece of clothesline from his mother's clothes pole. Andy Didio, whose father is an electrician, brought along a big spool of wire. Seth Snyder supplied some rope he'd found in the basement. Hambone Reilly was carrying around a four-foot length of heavy steel cable; I didn't figure we could do much with it, but Hambone's heart was in the right place.

The day before, when I'd talked to the kids, I'd asked the girls to bring some fabric to cover the kite. Rosalie Ippoliti brought a bright orange bedspread she'd found on a shelf. Sue Long, looking pretty as a picture, provided some living room drapes she said she hoped her mother didn't want anymore. Knobby Knees Knobel brought six feet of purple fabric she'd found in her mother's sewing room.

Stumps Peden had brought some smaller boards. Joey and I sawed them to length to make cross braces. We should have measured them, but we'd forgotten to bring a yardstick, so Joey eyeballed them.

Did you know that identical twins can read each other's minds? Brady Aldrich held the cross braces while Grady nailed them in place. They did it without saying a word to each other.

The framework took shape pretty fast. Joey's eyeball hadn't been accurate, though, so it didn't look square. In fact, when Grady tried to put in the last nail, Brady had to stand on the stick to force it into place.

We stood back and looked at the framework. There wasn't a straight board in it. Even the main sticks had been sprung out of shape.

"It won't fly," I said.

"Sure it will," said Joey. There was a ring of confidence in his voice. "Nail on the covering. Then we'll give it a test flight."

"Hallelujah!" said Timmy Belasco, sitting in his coaster wagon nearby. "Hallelujah, bring on the marines!" It was Timmy's favorite expression. He was shivering. I wondered why, because it wasn't cold.

Rosalie stepped forward with her orange bedspread, and Sue unfolded her living room drapes. The Aldrich twins started nailing the fabric to the framework. It didn't go on straight, of course. Angela Hibbs, looking even prettier than Sue Long, got out the Swiss

Army knife her grandfather gave her for Christmas, and used the little folding scissors to trim the fabric.

We ran out of bedspread and drapes, so Knobby Knees unrolled the purple cloth from her mother's sewing room and we went to work on it. Very pretty stuff, all soft and shiny. Must have been expensive.

By now Joey was as excited as a fox in a henhouse, running around that goofy kite and shouting instructions to anyone who would listen. I've never heard him talk so much.

At one point he stopped in his tracks and lifted his face toward the sky. He sniffed twice. "Wind's coming up!" he declared with authority. (First time I ever knew anybody could *smell* the wind.) "May be getting too strong. Prepare for launch!"

I lined up everybody who had brought rope or wire, and had them tie all the pieces together. It made a strange-looking pile there on the ground.

Stumps Peden trotted toward me. "My father was in the navy and taught me how to coil a rope. Want me to do it?"

"You betcha," I said. "Hurry up."

There was no question that Stumps knew what he was doing. In spite of the knobby knots all through our kite "string," Stumps carefully coiled it in a nice big circle on the ground, loop over loop. It was the only nice-looking thing on Oostermeyer's field except for Angela Hibbs, who's been my secret girl since last December. That's when I watched her recite "The Boy

Stood on the Burning Deck" during the Christmas program. Sue Long is the only one who gives Angela any competition in my secret dreams. I get goose bumps all over when I look at Angela.

Joey studied the plans, scratching his nose like he always does when he's deep in thought. "We need a bridle," he said.

From all the other kites we'd built I knew exactly how important a bridle can be. I tied a piece of rope to the top and bottom of one of the sticks, leaving plenty of slack. Then I tied the end of the big coil of rope to the bridle.

By now the wind had come up stronger, probably blowing in a storm. Except for the moan of the wind, it was strangely quiet. I heard a couple of cars *shiiiiiiiish* by on Highway 12, and the snort of Oostermeyer's bull in the next field.

Joey pulled on the leather gloves he'd brought along. Half a dozen kids were holding the kite on its side in the field. Joey took a deep breath and nodded to me.

I pulled Timmy's wagon over to one side, where he'd be out of the way. "Everybody take hold of the kite," I ordered. "When I count to three, set the kite right side up. Then I'll count to three again, and everybody push it straight up and let go."

Joey uncoiled about twenty feet of the rope, and backed off until it was taut.

"One!" I shouted, hanging on to one of the studs. My voice trembled. "Two! Three!"

We all pivoted the kite upright. Instantly a gust of wind hit it. I was sure we were going to lose control. Beside me, Grady dug in his heels, and on the other side of the kite Brady pushed against the force of the wind.

"Pull!" shouted Grady.

"Push!" shouted Brady.

"One!" I hollered. "Two! THREE!"

We heaved the kite up toward the sky.

The World's Largest Box Kite was an instant success. It shot up like a rocket off a launchpad.

I glanced back at Joey. He was trying to stop the rope, but the kite was too strong for him. The rope whistled right on through his gloves. Good thing they were thick leather. I wouldn't have been surprised if they'd started smoking, that rope was moving so fast.

Above my head, the kite was making a groaning noise, along with loud pops and cracks. One corner of the purple material had come loose and was snapping in the wind. The kite looked spectacular, wheeling back and forth as it climbed. The living room drapes seemed almost fluorescent against the light of the gray sky.

Joey was still struggling to gain control of the rope. Every time he'd slow it down a new gust of wind would hit the kite, and away she'd go again.

"Help!" he shouted.

I ran toward him, along with Stumps and the Aldrich twins.

We almost made it.

I'll never know what got into Joey. When I asked him about it later, he didn't have any explanation. He glanced down at the rope and found the last knot passing through his gloves. All that remained beyond that knot was Willie Duff's mother's clothesline. For some reason, Joey wouldn't let the knot pass through his gloves. He dug in his heels, and held on to that knot like his hands were frozen to it.

Joey Gootz rose right up into the sky.

No kidding, it was like a magician I saw over at the Coliseum in Center City; he made a woman float right out over the audience. One moment Joey was digging his heels into the ground, and the next moment he was sailing above my head, going higher every second.

I grabbed for the end of the clothesline at the same time Stumps did, and we bonked heads. I saw stars, but managed to hold on to the rope. Stumps did the same, and within seconds the Aldrich twins had come to our aid.

"Hallelujah!" shouted Timmy Belasco. "Bring on the marines!"

I looked up. Joey was dangling at least thirty feet off the ground, swinging wildly back and forth. His eyes were bigger than the rest of his face. Way out beyond him, the World's Largest Box Kite swooped back and forth across the sky like a giant orange-and-purple eagle.

"HANG ON!" I hollered at Joey.

"Pull him back!" shouted Grady in my ear.

We tried pulling Joey in, but didn't make much progress. About all we managed to do was walk backward across the field, which made the kite rise higher in the sky. Joey, too.

A terrible new worry flashed through my mind: How strong was Willie Duff's mother's clothesline? If it snapped, Joey was a goner.

Because we were pulling backward against the gusty wind, the kite began making huge swoops across the sky. It raced madly downward in one direction, then veered back up and swooped down in the opposite direction.

Joey swung like a pendulum. I knew he couldn't last much longer. His life flashed before my eyes.

Suddenly the wind stopped blowing as though it was completely out of breath.

At that moment a new disaster loomed. The kite came fluttering toward the ground, gaining speed every second.

Joey was doing an incredible job of hanging on, but now it didn't seem to matter. He would be a goner as soon as he hit the ground. I ran toward the spot where he'd most likely come down. I screeched to a stop when I saw Noah Oostermeyer's bull.

I felt a gust of wind on the side of my face. Joey came screaming down within three feet of the bull's horns, then popped skyward again in the gust of wind.

For such a little kid, Joey sure did scare that bull.

It was just as though the fence wasn't there. The bull came charging through, and fence posts and barbed wire flew in every direction.

We were right in front of his charge. He headed toward us like an ugly black locomotive, the ground shaking under his hooves. Above my head, I could hear the kite groaning and popping, and Joey screeching at the top of his voice.

As long as I live I'll never forget the sight of that bull. His big head was black as Satan. His eyes were huge and watery, and his nostrils about the size of Pop's coffee cup. The shiny black horns curved upward and outward to tips that looked as sharp as needles.

Joey has been my best friend for as long as I can remember. I'm ashamed to say that his friendship didn't matter right now. In fact, I forgot all about Joey. I dropped the rope and ran for my life. When I heard the bull's hooves right behind me, I dived to the ground. I heard other kids thudding all around.

Lying there in the field, I heard a roar like a jet engine, and a big hoof smashed down six inches from my nose. It disappeared in a flash.

I counted to three, then scrambled to my feet. The bull was thundering off toward the far end of the field. Kids were lying all around. Rosalie had her face in her hands. Stumps rolled his head back and forth.

"Hallelujah!" said Timmy Belasco. He was lying under his coaster wagon. "Hallelujah! Hallelujah!"

Angela Hibbs was looking straight at me, eyes wide

and a moan coming from her lips. I started over to comfort her.

Then I remembered Joey.

Joey!

I swung around and looked up into the sky. The morning sun was just breaking through the clouds, and for a couple of winks I couldn't spot either Joey or the kite.

Then I saw them both.

If you've ever flown a regular-size kite, you know what happens when the string breaks. The kite flutters slowly down out of the sky. The same thing happened to the World's Largest Box Kite.

It sailed down like a wounded bird. A loose corner of the orange bedspread flapped in the wind.

When Joey came closer, I could tell from the anguished look on his face that his strength was gone. As he approached the ground he picked up speed. It looked as though he'd hit like a bomb, but at the last moment the kite gave a friendly little flutter in a sudden gust of wind.

Joey landed as light as a feather, but moving like mad toward the North Pole.

One second he was dangling above the ground, and the next second he could easily have outrun every wide receiver in the National Football League.

It was a superhuman effort, but Joey's legs just couldn't run fast enough to keep up with the rest of him. He sprawled flat on his face.

I figured he was knocked out, but when I came running up he flopped over on his back and fluttered his eyes at me. He made a strangled sound deep in his throat.

"You all right?" I asked anxiously.

His face was as white as a Sunday handkerchief, except for a blob of dirt where he'd buried his nose in the field. Rattling sounds tumbled out of his mouth.

He nodded his head.

Then, incredibly, he grinned. "World's Largest Box Kite," he croaked.

THE WORLD'S LARGEST BOX KITE.

This monster kite was built by Joey Gootz and his Fairfield friends, and measured more than twelve feet high. On June 14 at 10:05 A.M. it made a spectacular flight, complete with a live passenger, over Oostermeyer's pasture. The remains of the kite now hang on the wall in Pop Potts's toolshed. I witnessed the event, and hereby swear that it is a new world's record.

Peter Potts

☆ 3 ☆

The World's Tallest and Fastest Stilt Walk

As I said before, Pop can be as mean as a cornered civet cat when he's in between hobbies and has nothing to occupy his mind.

Early last summer he was mean for two weeks. He'd suddenly gone out of the business of "Raising Giant South African Land Crabs for Fun and Profit." It was all a mistake—after feeding the crabs one night, Pop forgot to close the gate on their pen.

The sight of freedom must have been too much for those huge critters. They walked sideways up the road into town. One grabbed Mrs. Smithers's prize Persian cat by the nose and flung it sixteen feet down Miller Street. Another crawled up on the front porch and grabbed Mr. Simpkins's gouty toe in a death lock. It took Police Chief Fuzzy Thurston and the volunteer fire department almost an hour to pry it loose. Mr. Simpkins hollered bloody murder.

Fuzzy Thurston was so busy rounding up Pop's

giant crabs that he had no time to arrest hardened criminals. It didn't matter; we hardly ever have any hardened criminals around Fairfield. Mainly Fuzzy directs traffic at funerals and settles arguments over fences. He ordered Pop to get rid of the crabs, so Pop shipped them back to the company he'd bought them from. Pop got steadily meaner for two weeks after that.

Then, right after the mail arrived on a Tuesday, I noticed Pop settling down in his easy chair with a package in his lap. He slit open the box with his pocketknife and pulled out a book. Within two minutes he was sucking air through the gap in his front teeth. Within five minutes it sounded like a jet plane was roaring through the living room. It was a dead-sure sign that he was excited.

Pop is about a foot shorter than most grown men. He has a walrus-style moustache that tends to strain the food he eats. He avoids corn on the cob.

"What's your new hobby?" I asked.

He looked across at me, a grin on his face. "Pete, you're looking at a famous man. At least I'll be famous within a week."

He held up the book so I could see the cover. The title was *Stilts and Stilt-Walking for the Serious Amateur*.

I walked over and leaned across the back of Pop's chair so I could see the pages of the book.

"See, Pete, this first chapter is on making a simple

pair of stilts from two oak branches. Here's a chapter on learning to walk on stilts. And here's another on how to use stilts like the circus clowns use—stilts that strap on to your legs and make you ten feet tall."

"That book is going to make you famous?" I couldn't believe it.

"Why, I'll be in demand for every parade in Fairfield, and every one in Center City as well. By jabbers, they'll probably send a TV crew to film me for the 'Nightly News' with Joe Billings and Millie Magraw. 'Fairfield man walks in the sky. Story at eleven.' "

What I like most about Pop is that he never dreams small dreams.

★   ★   ★

Two days later I began to think that Pop was right— he was destined to become famous. Joey and I came up the driveway about noon in search of a peanut butter and jelly sandwich. Pop was clomping across the front yard on a pair of stilts that made him about eight feet tall.

When he saw us he let out a whoop and broke into a fast trot toward us. I thought he was going to stomp us to death, but at the last second he veered to the right, then did a little dance behind us. He was singing "Bad, Bad Leroy Brown" at the top of his voice. At the end of the second verse he jumped off the stilts and landed right in front of us. The stilts clattered to the driveway.

"Wow!" was all I could say.

"Amazing!" There was awe in Joey's voice.

"I knew it!" exclaimed Pop. "I'm a natural born stilt-walker, and with a little more practice I'll be the best in the biz." His eyes were flashing, and air whistled through his teeth.

★   ★   ★

We'd finished our sandwiches, and Pop was trying to find where Betts had hidden her molasses cookies so they'd last two days instead of just one. "Doggone that girl!" he said. "Ever since she found out a baby is on its way, she can't keep her mind on the more important things of life."

Exactly my own feelings. That morning Betts had refused to play catch with me. When I asked her why, she blamed it on "morning sickness." When I asked her what "morning sickness" meant, she said I'd never understand until I had it myself, and that wasn't very likely during my lifetime. I reminded her how sick I got the morning Joey dared me to eat half a dozen live ants. Now, *that's* what I call "morning sickness."

Betts immediately got a very strange look on her face, ran for the bathroom, and locked herself in. It was obvious she didn't want to have any further conversation with me. Now here we were, not talking to each other for the first time in our lives, and we probably never would play catch together again. Somehow a tiny bit of life inside Betts had changed our lives drastically.

Anyway, Joey and I had finished our sandwiches, and Pop was poking around the back of the breadbox trying to find the cookies. Joey suddenly lifted his head and looked across the table at me. His eyes were glazed over, and he was scratching his nose with his left forefinger.

"World's Tallest Stilts," he said in a low voice.

"How's that?" asked Pop. He was down on his hands and knees grubbing around behind the refrigerator.

"The World's Tallest Stilts," I repeated in a voice loud enough for Pop to hear.

There was a moment of silence. Then Pop scrambled to his feet, eyes dancing. "Joey, that's one of the greatest ideas of the century. Bound to make me famous. I may even do a command performance at the White House."

"How'll we make the World's Tallest Stilts?" I asked.

"We'll need something long—maybe about fifteen feet—and perfectly straight." Joey was thinking out loud.

"And lightweight," put in Pop. "If I'm going to walk on them, I have to lift them with my legs, and the longer they are the heavier they'll be."

"Balsa wood?" Joey asked. "Like we make model airplanes out of?"

Pop snorted. "Too soft. Anyway, where would you

get balsa boards fifteen feet long? You'd have to order them special from South America, or wherever. That would take months, and we want to break the world's record this afternoon."

I slapped my hand on the table. "Got it! There's a new kind of plastic pipe stacked in front of the Bildmore Lumberyard. It's strong, straight, and fairly lightweight."

"By cricket, Pete, that might do the job."

"Do we have enough money for two pieces?" I asked.

To tell the truth, I was trying to protect my savings account. When Betts first told me about the baby, I got all hotted up over the idea of having a brand-new nephew. I started putting some money in the bank every week to buy him a welcome-into-the-world present. I liked to read the column of figures in my savings account book; the neat line of numbers gave me a warm feeling just above the top of my stomach. Now, I had some different feelings about the baby, but not about my bank account. Being a pretty good guy, I'd probably still spend some of it on my nephew, but it was going to hurt. Oh, well. Nobody likes a penny-pinching uncle. That's a good thought for the day.

"My treat," said Pop. "I'll pay for the pipe. Let's go get it right now." He headed for the door, then stopped in his tracks. He stooped over, reached far to the back of the bottom cabinet, and pulled out Betts's turkey-roasting pan, which she uses once a year, on

Thanksgiving. He jerked off the lid, reached inside, and pulled out a plastic container filled with molasses cookies.

"That granddaughter of mine is clever," he said in triumph. "But she'll never outfox her grandfather."

★ ★ ★

We rattled back from Bildmore with two fifteen-foot sections of plastic pipe bouncing around in the bed of Pop's old pickup truck. You may not know how long fifteen feet is. It's about as long as three and one-half fifth-graders laid end to end.

Joey cut some steps, for Pop's feet, out of a two-by-four. Pop drilled some holes about two feet from one end of each pipe, and bolted the steps to the pipe.

Joey was getting as excited as an ant that's accidentally crawled across a hot pancake griddle. He looked up at Pop. "How you planning to hold on to the stilts?" he asked.

Pop scratched his ear. "I'll stand on the stilt steps," he said, "and you boys strap the pipe tight to my legs with some clothesline. Then I'll step off briskly, and we'll be in business."

"A new world's record!" Joey said proudly, as though the championship event had already occurred. He picked up the stilts, carried them outside, and dropped them on the ground.

"Not so fast," I said. There's no question I was the most practical person around the toolshed that day when you consider the inborn natures of Joey Gootz and Pop Potts. "How are we going to get you upright, Pop?"

"What do you mean?" Pop spoke defensively. "Speak plain, Pete."

"Okay. Look at the stilts, lying there on the ground. You can lie down on your back beside them, and we can tie them to your legs with your feet on the steps. Now you're ready to go, except that you're *lying* there. How do we tilt you up so you can walk?"

Pop scratched his ear again. "Good thinking, Pete. You put your finger on a real problem."

Joey eyeballed the stilts, thinking deep thoughts. "We could take them over to Noah Oostermeyer's barn," he suggested. "You could climb up in the haymow, we could strap on the stilts, and then you could walk away from the barn."

"No!" Pop said decisively. "Noah Oostermeyer wouldn't lend me one of his pigs for my animal training experiments, so I'm not letting him in on this world's record."

"How's this for an idea?" I said. "Joey and I take a piece of rope upstairs to my room and lower it out the window. Pop, you lie down on the ground and we'll strap you onto the stilts. The bottom of the stilts will be against the house. We'll tie the rope to your belt. Then Joey and I will go upstairs, haul the rope up through the window, and you'll pivot right up to the window yourself."

"By cricket that's a pretty good idea, Pete. It's obvious you came from a bright family. Let's do it!"

Ten minutes later we were ready to set the world's record. A piece of rope was tied to the head of my bed, and dangled out the window to the ground. The stilts were lying on the ground straight out from the side of the house, and Pop's legs were strapped to them with pieces of Betts's clothesline. His feet were tied to the little steps.

Pop lay there on his back, grinning up at me, as I tied the rope from the window to his belt buckle. His eyes were snapping, and the air rushed through the gap in his teeth.

"Tomorrow, after I've practiced a bit, we'll call the TV station. By jabbers, I'll be the biggest local news story of the year!"

Joey was upstairs in my bedroom. He leaned out the window and pulled on the rope. Pop's back eased off the ground.

"Wait'll I come up and help!" I called.

I ran up the stairs two at a time, and joined Joey at the window. We both took hold of the rope and braced one foot against the windowsill.

"Ready, Pop?" I called down.

"Ready!" His voice was a croak.

Joey and I hauled. I was looking down at Pop. We almost broke his back when his hips came off the ground and his head didn't. His arms flailed until his hands brushed the rope. He grabbed it with both hands.

We hauled in the rope as fast as we could.

Actually, the whole thing worked even better than I'd hoped. Pop came rising right up to the window like he was on a well-greased track.

When he was about six feet away I could see his eyes snapping out of the wrinkles that ran every which way across his face. His straw hat fell off and fluttered to the ground. He was biting his lower lip so hard it was white as hog lard.

At that moment Joey's foot slipped off the windowsill. When he tried to recover his balance he lost his hold on the rope.

I tried to hang on.

Pop's face gradually disappeared from the window. I felt myself being pulled right out after him.

Joey finally recovered his balance and grabbed the rope. Together, we hauled Pop back up to the window.

There was a smile of triumph on Pop's face. He let go of the rope and grabbed the sides of the window frame.

"By jabbers, we're doing it. I'm standing here on the World's Tallest Stilts!"

"Can't call it a world's record yet." Joey's voice was serious and decisive. "You've got to *walk* on the stilts before we can claim a record."

Pop took a deep breath. "Okay! Here goes!"

"Wait!" I said. "If I'm going to witness this world's record, I want to do it from down on the ground."

Pop was steady as a rock now. He stood upright

on the stilts, hanging on to both sides of the bedroom window.

I untied the rope from his belt so it wouldn't be in his way when he took his first steps. Then Joey and I ran downstairs and out onto the lawn.

Pop made quite a sight standing there with his back to us, his face inside the bedroom window. The stilts were bending under his weight; he looked like a bow-legged stork.

"Okay!" I hollered.

Pop stepped backward, away from the side of the house. He swooped a little to his right, so he took a short step with his right leg to keep his balance. Then he straightened up and walked right across the lawn.

"Wow!" I shouted.

Joey was jumping up and down, a grin the size of a jack-o'-lantern on his face.

"I swear," Pop hollered from twenty feet in the air, "I could hike all the way to Center City."

Just then he veered off to the left without meaning to, and walked straight into our apple tree. His arms flailed through the leaves. One of the branches whacked him across the eyes.

That's when disaster struck. And I mean *total* disaster.

I saw the hornet's nest fall out of the tree and hit the ground.

Pop took a step backward to escape the branches, one hand rubbing his eyes. I could tell he was almost blind. One of his stilts crunched right down on that hornet's nest. It was like an explosion.

Joey started running up the driveway. I closed my eyes and froze. When in the vicinity of mad hornets, the best thing you can do is nothing. Just stand absolutely still. You might want to remember that. It could be a vitally important thought for the day.

Pop knew about standing perfectly still around angry hornets, of course, because he was the one who had taught it to me. But he had a major problem. *On stilts, you can't stand still.*

I opened my eyes and looked up at him, high above my head. The first hornet got him smack in the middle of the forehead.

He shouted "Uggggle Mugggle!" or something like that, swatting with one hand while he took a couple of steps, fighting for his balance.

Within thirty seconds there was a black cloud of hornets around Pop's head. I could see the tears streaming down his face. He took off like he was shot out of a cannon. Within two steps he was in full gear. And what steps! I'll bet he covered twenty feet each time a stilt struck the ground.

He headed up the driveway in the same direction Joey had disappeared, crossed Highway 12, and ran down County Road. I ran after him. Luckily all the hornets were around his head, not mine.

By the time I reached County Road, Pop was fifty

yards away, Joey running just ahead of him. Joey is fast on his feet, but Pop passed him like he was standing still. Every time Pop took a giant step the stilt kicked up a puff of dust.

County Road goes down a steep hill and curves past the millpond. Pop started down that hill lickety-split.

Every kid who has run down a steep hill knows that you can move your legs only so fast. Pretty soon your body is moving faster than your legs. At that point your body leans forward, your legs make one last effort to keep up, and you fall flat on your face.

By the time Joey and I got halfway down the hill Pop was almost at the bottom. Those long stilts were swinging so fast they were almost invisible. There was some give to those bowlegged stilts, and they gave Pop a kind of jump with each step, as though he was running on springs.

His body started to tip forward. I knew what was happening.

Just as he reached the bottom of the hill, the best thing in the world that could have happened did happen. His giant legs just couldn't keep up with his skinny little body. He took one final stride, compressing the stilts, and then his body took off like he was on a giant pogo stick. I could hear him holler as he sailed ten feet through the air.

The good thing that happened to Pop was that the

millpond was right there waiting for him. He hit with one of the worst bellyflops I've ever seen. Water splatted in every direction.

Joey and I could hardly breathe by the time we reached the edge of the millpond. Pop's bald head was sticking out of the water. There were at least a dozen bumps across his scalp, and his eyes were swollen almost shut. But there wasn't a hornet in sight. You might want to remember that water helps if you ever find yourself in a similar situation.

"Get me out of here!" he shouted. "Can't swim with these consarn stilts on!"

I waded out and grabbed the bottom of one stilt. Joey got hold of the other. We pulled Pop to shore and beached him.

He lay there like a bluegill that's been swung up onto land. He looked up at me, then over at Joey. We couldn't see his eyes because they were so swollen.

"By jabbers," he said, "a new world's record!"

"Yeah," I said. "For height and speed."

THE WORLD'S TALLEST
AND FASTEST STILT WALK.

The record was set by Pop Potts at his farm on the edge of Fairfield, Saturday, June 28. This assault on the world's record was suggested by Joey Gootz, and aided by the undersigned. The stilts are

now part of the drainage system under
the Potts back porch. I witnessed the
event, and hereby swear that it is a new
world's record.

Peter Potts

The World's Biggest Kid Parade

Fourth of July was a day so hot and rainy that the raindrops seemed to sizzle when they hit the pavement. It's unusual for us to have rain on the Fourth; midsummer is usually dry as dust around Fairfield. Farmers hereabouts go crazy in rainy weather; they don't have anything to complain about.

Sometime in the middle of the morning Joey and I came home from racing stickboats down the creek. Betts made us take off our clothes on the back porch because we were so muddy. Just shows you how she was acting more and more like a mother, now that she was going to become one.

I'd won most of the stickboat races and had come home in a good frame of mind. That didn't last long.

When we came into the kitchen, Betts and Mike were sitting at the table. Mike was talking while Betts made a long list on a sheet of paper.

"In addition to the bassinet and the six-year crib,"

Mike was saying, "we'll need some kind of a table for putting on his diapers. Don't they make a special thing just for that?"

"They call it a dressing table," said Betts. "We'll need plenty of diapers, of course. Sarah Short told me to get at least four dozen."

I got down a box of sugared Loopy Loops, poured some in Joey's outstretched hands, and put some in my mouth. Betts and Mike didn't seem to realize we were in the room.

"I'll get your grandmother's rocking chair from the attic," said Mike. "Every baby needs to be rocked."

"Good idea, dear. Let's see. We'll need a baby bathtub, and a chest of drawers. And before long we'll want a high chair, a playpen, and a potty training seat." She added them to her list.

A potty training seat!

"I was looking in Radio Shack yesterday," said Mike. "They've got a gadget—really a radio transmitter—that you put in the baby's room when the baby goes to sleep. You take the receiver with you, wherever you go, and you can hear any noise the baby makes, even its breathing."

I exploded. "You talk about buying that kid a two-way walkie-talkie radio before it's even born, and I've never had one in all of my life! Not even for Christmas!" I shouted the last words, and pieces of Loopy Loops went flying across the kitchen.

An anguished look passed across Betts's face. She

got up so quickly that her chair crashed backward against the wall. For a moment she stood there, looking at me through sudden tears, then walked over and put her arms around me.

I guess there were tears in my eyes, too, but I still was mad as a billygoat. "This stuff you're buying for the baby"—I asked through a tight throat—"where are you going to put all of it?"

Betts instantly tightened her arms around me.

There was a long silence. Then Mike cleared his throat. "We thought you and I might work together, Pete, fixing up the back bedroom exactly the way you want it. We'll cover the walls with brand new paneling, and I'll help put up shelves wherever you want them."

"The back bedroom," I said into Betts's shoulder. I wasn't shouting now. "The small bedroom." The words were a whisper.

"Pete, you don't have to move," she said softly. "You can stay right where you are. That room is your room forever, if you want it. We just thought it takes so many *things* to take care of a baby, maybe you might want to—" Her voice trailed off.

I stepped away without looking into her face. Joey was standing in the corner, looking as though he'd been watching McGoldrick's big Siamese cat in a spitting fight with Howlett's bulldog.

"I'll think about it," I said. I motioned Joey to follow me.

We went into the living room in our undershorts. Pop was watching the big Fourth of July parade on TV. He's a sucker for a parade of any kind. Just strike up a band—any band—and he's on the march. If he can't march, he wants to watch. He was scheduled to drive the volunteer fire truck in the Fairfield parade that afternoon, but it looked like the paraders would be marching through a thunderstorm.

"Wow! Look at that!" said Joey. He plopped down on the floor and propped his head between his hands.

A marching band was turning itself inside out, then doubling back to tie itself in knots. It was all very complicated, and you'd swear they'd never straighten out the mess, when suddenly ten girls waving batons and wearing not much but smiles appeared from the middle of the mess and led the reformed band down the street. It was amazing. I eased off being mad at Betts, just a bit.

"Mighty fine band," said Pop, reaching for a pretzel. "One of the best parades I've ever seen, and one of the biggest."

I glanced over at Joey. His eyes were glazing over and he was scratching his nose. I bonked him on the head with my elbow. His eyelids batted once or twice, and he looked up at me.

"The World's Biggest Parade," he said.

"C'mon, Joey," I said. "How are you going to get together a parade bigger than the one on TV right now?"

"Not sure yet," he said, sitting up. Then his voice grew more firm. "It'll be a kids' parade. Every kid in Fairfield. And maybe some from Center City and every other town in this part of the state. Biggest kids' band ever assembled, too. Another world's record." Joey was on a roll.

"You're out of your skull. What will the kids use for instruments?"

"Whatever they want to play. They'll bring their own instruments. And we'll have clowns and jugglers, acrobats and other performers by the thousands. Biggest parade the world has ever seen. All kids."

Pop sucked air through the gap in his teeth. He was getting excited, too. "You got an idea that's a head-buster, Joey. The World's Biggest Parade. Has a mighty nice ring to it."

"How are you going to get all these zillions of kids involved?" I asked, trying to bring Pop and Joey down to earth.

"Publicity," Joey answered. He was already a dozen thoughts ahead of me. "Every kid for a hundred miles around Fairfield will hear about it, and won't be able to resist. Publicity—that's the secret."

"If you want publicity," said Pop, "go see Willy Peters."

It was just naturally a great idea. Willy Peters seems to loaf his way through life, but money drifts from other folks' pockets into his. Mostly that happens because Willy gets them excited about something. That's what's called publicity.

"Willy won't have anything to do with our parade," I objected, "unless we pay him for it."

"That's almost true, but not quite." Pop popped another pretzel into his mouth. "What you really mean is that Willy won't publicize your parade unless he can see some money in it for himself. And that's Willy's greatest talent—spotting ways to make money off other people's work."

Pop should know. Willy once made a fortune when Pop took up lion taming for a hobby.

Joey jumped to his feet. "Let's go find Willy." He can't let a world's record stand idle.

We went out on the porch, put on our muddy clothes, and bicycled through the rain into town.

★　★　★

When he's not busy making money, Willy Peters hangs out at Tremont's Barber and Billiard Shop. It's the only place I know of where you can get your hair cut while watching the best pool sharks in three states. Tremont's stays open all day every day of the year, and every night until the last customer goes home.

Betts won't let me go into Tremont's anymore. She says there are evil influences there, and that it's not the right kind of place for a child. She never worried about that until she got pregnant and began reading books on the right way to raise children. She seems to think I'm going to be an evil influence on the baby, just by walking into Tremont's. Peter Potts, the Evil Influence! Anyway, Betts now cuts my hair herself. I wonder if she'll still have time to cut it after the brat arrives. Maybe I'll turn out to be the Long-Haired Evil Influence of Fairfield.

I followed Joey into Tremont's. Mr. Tremont, in his white barber jacket, was brushing sweet-smelling powder across the back of Steve Krohmer's neck. He glanced up and frowned. He didn't like kids in his place unless they were there for a haircut.

Billiard balls clicked. I glanced over at the pool table. Two guys who work out at the chicken factory were intent on their game. Willy Peters was watching. He was sitting in a chair that was tilted back against the wall. He wore a fancy plaid jacket over a gold vest. Willy once told me that you have to *look* wealthy to *get* wealthy. That's a good thought for the day if you have a sincere interest in getting wealthy.

Joey walked over and stood in front of the tilted chair. His pants were covered with mud thrown up by his bicycle wheels. He looked like a peasant approaching the throne.

"Hi, Willy," he said.

"Hello, Joey." He looked across at me. "Hi, Pete. What's Pop up to these days? Any new hobbies?"

"Nothing you'd be interested in," I said, thinking of Pop's disaster on the stilts.

"You never know what I might be interested in."

"That's why we're here," piped up Joey. "We've got a great idea, and we thought you might give us some advice on how to publicize it. It might make a lot of money." Joey must have thrown that last thought in as bait.

"Money does come in handy. What's your idea?"

"The World's Biggest Parade. All kids. Think of it, Willy!"

There was a long silence, broken by the click of the billiard balls.

Willy repeated Joey's words: "The World's Biggest Parade." The front legs of his chair slammed down against the floor. "I like the idea right off the bat," he said. "It would put Fairfield on the map. How do you boys plan to go about organizing it?"

"That's why we're here," said Joey. "We need your help."

"We want to get hundreds, maybe thousands of kids in the parade," I explained. "To do that we need publicity. We thought you might tell us how to get it."

A smile passed across Willy's face. With one finger he smoothed down his neat little moustache. "So you boys are here to consult Willy Peters Enterprises."

My heart sank. That's what Willy calls his money-making schemes. Already he was putting our discussion on a business basis.

"I guess so," I said. But right away I added, "We

don't have any money to pay for your advice, Willy."

He looked sharply at me. "That's not the point, Pete. The point is not whether you have money, but *whether money can be made off your idea*. Are you boys willing to give me a hundred-percent share of any profits?"

How can a hundred percent be a share? I thought. I glanced at Joey. He nodded.

"Okay," I said. "Give us some advice."

He sat there in silence for a full minute, rubbing down his moustache. Then he said, "Posters. Newspaper stories. Radio. TV from Center City. Try for network coverage."

I was staggered. We hadn't been thinking on this scale. "We can put up posters, Willy. But how do we get stories in the newspaper?"

"Herb Sachs owes me a favor." He made it sound mysterious. Herb Sachs is the editor of the *Fairfield Clarion*, which comes out twice a week. "And we'll plant a story in the *Center City Gazette*."

"Radio?" asked Joey.

"We might buy a few spots. WBZZ gives a special rate to Willy Peters Enterprises."

"It'll still take money," said Joey. "Where do we get it?"

"Let me worry about that. The profit potential in your idea, Joey, is fairly high."

"There's no way we can get TV publicity," I declared flatly. "We're just a couple of kids with a far-out idea."

"Let me ask you boys one question. Do you ever watch 'Stars of Tomorrow' on Channel 4?"

I hit my forehead with the heel of my hand. Dumb. That's what I was. Of course I watch the program. Fairfield isn't big enough to have its own TV station, so everybody watches Channel 4 from Center City. Every Saturday morning, while their parents are sleeping late, the kids get up and watch Dan Miner present "Stars of Tomorrow."

It's an absolutely crazy program. Kids stand there in front of the camera, and in front of other kids, and do anything they want. Some kids play violins and recite poems and all that kind of junk, but other kids put on acts that just knock you out. I've seen a boy juggle live chickens, and a girl jump rope with her dog. I've seen kids do imitations of everything from a typewriter to Superman zapping the Emperor of the Evil Empire.

Ickey Icke went over to Center City from Fairfield and did his rubber-mask act on "Stars of Tomorrow." Ickey has flimsy skin almost everywhere on his head, and he can pull and shove it into fifteen different faces that would petrify a mule. Ickey was such a success that his friend Herman Schnitz took his bouncing dog over for the next week's program. Hermy's dog bounces straight up and down like a rubber ball until Hermy tells it to stop. Sometimes the dog is difficult to get back under control, and goes bouncing off on its own. Anyway, kids all over our part of the state watch the program every Saturday morning.

I looked at Joey. His eyes were shining.

"Tell us what to do, Willy," I said.

★　★　★

Pop was as excited as we were about the progress we were making. Now we needed the personal touch. Early the next Saturday morning we piled into Pop's pickup truck and headed for Center City.

Willy had made some phone calls during the week, arranging for Joey and me to appear on "Stars of Tomorrow." He'd given us long rehearsals on what to say in front of the cameras. He seemed to lean a little heavily on me; he must know Joey is a boy of few words.

We arrived at the studio about half an hour before program time. We gave a blond lady in a short skirt our names, and she directed us through the second door on the right.

When we opened that door we walked into an absolute zoo. Kids were shouting and running everywhere. One girl in a fancy pink dress was sitting in a corner tuning her cello, her head bowed to one side to listen, when a bowling pin flung by a teenage juggler hit her on the right ear. A kid walked in front of me carrying a screened box that held about fifty white mice. A six-year-old was sailing to the ceiling off a miniature trampoline.

There were cameras and lights all around. On a stage at one end of the room, a young man with a neatly trimmed black beard was seated at a desk, smiling happily down at the chaos below. I recognized him instantly: Dan Miner, Talentmaster of "Stars of Tomorrow." By his right elbow was his famous gong. It announced each act, and if you were in the middle of your act when the gong *bong*ed, your act was over. Period.

I punched Joey on the shoulder, and we forced our way over to the three steps that led up to the stage.

Dan Miner gave us his famous toothy smile when we walked up to his desk. No matter how hard you try, you fall apart when you meet someone in person that you've seen countless times on TV.

"Potts!" I shouted over the noise in the studio. "I'm Peter Potts. And this is Joey Gootz." Dan Miner looked down at a paper on his desk. "Yep," he said in his familiar bass voice. "Gotcha. Kids from Fairfield. What's that rascal Willy Peters up to these days?"

It shook me up that this famous TV star was a friend of Willy.

Dan Miner didn't seem to expect a reply. "Willy told me you boys have one of the world's greatest ideas. He was very mysterious. If it's good enough for Willy, it's good enough for me. Let's see. Gotcha listed right after Weezie the Girl Yodeler." He smiled through his teeth again to dismiss us. We trotted back down the steps.

A few minutes later the gong sounded through the chaos. Dan Miner hammed it up for about thirty seconds. Gradually the kids in the studio quieted down, sitting on the floor around the studio, just as I'd seen them do on TV.

Dan Miner pointed to a small glass panel in the wall beside his desk. "When you see that light go on," he announced, "it means we're on the air. Keep quiet, except when you're applauding. You can clap and yell, if you like, at the end of any act. Otherwise keep quiet." He looked at the big clock over his desk. "Thirty seconds to air time."

We waited expectantly. The light went on.

Dan Miner's face became all teeth. "Welcome to 'Stars of Tomorrow'!"

He talked for a minute about how talented kids are, then introduced the first act, called Fast Eddie and his Singing Dog. Fast Eddie didn't do anything except wave a baton at a spotted dog while a woman played "It Ain't Gonna Rain No More, No More" on the piano. The dog was kind of a mangy little mutt, but it was a pretty good singer. Every time Fast Eddie waved his baton, the dog barked.

At the end of the song, the dog's howl climbed up to a real high note. All of us clapped and hooted. Fast Eddie bowed like *he'd* done something special.

The second act wasn't much, until right at the end. Bouncing Betty was about nine years old, and for two minutes she bounced around the platform on her pogo stick. Right at the end, though, she got going higher and higher, and then suddenly she did a full cartwheel in midair and landed on her stick, still bouncing. I swear it. We were all so surprised we almost forgot to applaud.

Bong! "Now it is my great pleasure to present Weezie the Yodeler."

Joey nudged me, and we edged up through the crowd until we stood right at the bottom of the steps. Just above us Weezie yodeled her heart out.

Bong!

"I understand that the next act is not really an act at all. But Joey Gootz and Peter Potts, from over in Fairfield, have a very important announcement to make. They are appearing here today courtesy of Willy Peters Enterprises." That was news to me. "Please give Joey and Peter your undivided attention."

Joey bounced up the steps. I followed, trying to put a Dan Miner–type smile on my face. Everybody clapped like mad, as though we'd already done something special. We sat down in the two chairs beside Dan Miner's desk. Dan looked at Joey.

"Now, Joey, what's this great mystery all about? What's this significant announcement you have to make?"

Joey's eyes kind of popped out of his headbones and glazed over like a Supersinker chocolate doughnut.

Dan Miner must have sensed immediately that he had a turkey on his hands, so he turned to me. "Peter? What do you have to say?"

I looked at the microphone hanging down above the desk. All of a sudden I thought of the thousands and thousands of kids watching me on their television sets. I tried to swallow, but there wasn't anything to swallow.

"Peter?"

I opened my mouth. "Murrrf." That's all I could say.

Everybody laughed, and a couple of kids started jeering.

That made me mad. "Shut up," I shouted. Suddenly I was on my feet. Out of the corner of my eye I saw Dan Miner pick up the drumstick to beat the gong.

"Don't do that!" I shouted. "Don't hit that gong, Mr. Miner. I've got something to say, and I'm going to say it."

Dan Miner's teeth appeared again. He put down the drumstick. "Go right ahead, Peter."

I swallowed, and this time some spit went down. "Joey and I came here to invite you to something special. Something *very* special. In Fairfield, next Saturday, at ten-thirty in the morning, we're going to have the World's Biggest Parade, led by the World's

Biggest Marching Band. There'll be hundreds, maybe thousands of kids there."

Joey jumped to his feet, eyes flashing. "Get listed in the book of world's records!" he shouted. "Tell 'em, Pete!"

It was then that I had one of the great inspirations of my life. If you look back on your life, now and then, you can find some things you've done that really make you proud. Not very many. But a few. That's a comforting thought.

"We're having the parade to raise money for a great cause," I said. I don't know why I lowered my voice, but I did, and suddenly the studio grew quiet. "We're going to help buy a kidney transplant for little Timmy Belasco."

Timmy had gone to the hospital the week before, even though both Joey and I knew his parents couldn't afford it. He was waiting there for a donated kidney. Then would come a very difficult and expensive operation.

Quietly I told the kids in the studio about Timmy. And I suddenly remembered that I was talking to a zillion other kids, too. I looked straight into the camera in front of me.

"Timmy is from Fairfield, but at this moment he's in the hospital right here in Center City, waiting for the kidney transplant that his parents can't afford. We're going to parade for Timmy Belasco! All of us! Every kid here! Every kid in the state! We're going to help pay for the operation to give Timmy a new kidney!"

"Band instruments. And pets." Joey whispered the words in my ear.

"If you play a musical instrument, bring it," I said. "If you don't play an instrument, bring a couple of pot lids to slam together, or a bucket you can beat on. If you don't want to do that, bring your pet, any kind of pet. If you don't have a pet, come along and do your own thing, whatever it is. Do it for Timmy Belasco! Are you with us?"

The crowd clapped.

I was still looking into the camera. "All of you kids out there watching on TV—you come, too. *Every one of you!* If you don't live in Fairfield, come anyway. Have your folks drive you to the Fairfield High School football field next Saturday morning. Arrive at ten o'clock. Guarantee your folks a parade like they've never seen before."

"Dan Miner!" Joey whispered in my ear.

Didn't I tell you Joey sometimes is a genius? I looked across at Dan. "And we're especially inviting you, Mr. Miner. You'll have time to drive over to Fairfield after next Saturday's program. We're asking you to be Grand Marshal of the biggest parade ever organized, the parade that will set a new world's record, the parade for Timmy Belasco. Will you agree to be our Grand Marshal?"

A shout rang through the studio.

Dan Miner nodded his head. What else could he do?

∗ ∗ ∗

I have to admit that Willy Peters did a masterful job of getting publicity for the parade. Every day, all through the week, there were articles in the *Fairfield Clarion* and the *Center City Gazette*. I was interviewed on our little local radio station. And Willy himself appeared on NBC nightly news, which gave us publicity all across the country.

Joey and I were dropping into the pool hall daily to confer with Willy. (Betts gave me fits about where I was "hanging out.") Things were rolling along so good that on Thursday, just two days before the parade, I said to Willy, "How come you're doing this, Willy? You know we don't have any money, and every penny we take in for the parade is going to help pay for Timmy Belasco's new kidney."

Willy rubbed down his moustache. "Don't you boys fret about Willy Peters," he said. "Willy looks out for himself."

I knew those words were the truth.

By now, Joey and I were beginning to worry about the parade. After all the ballyhoo, what if nobody showed up? On the other hand, what if a thousand kids showed up and we had no way of controlling them?

Kids are funny; some kids behave normally because

that's what they *want* to do, and some kids go hog wild because that's what *they* want to do. That's an extra free thought for the day.

On Thursday night Joey had a nightmare about the hog wild–type kids. His hands shook as he told me about it. There were a zillion kids in his dream, and all were tearing Fairfield apart. Joey tried to shout at them to stop, but he couldn't force out more than a whisper. Finally he gave one shout, and they all turned toward him. They started chasing him. Fortunately he woke up before they caught him.

Joey's nightmare taught us we needed some way to control the crowd—if any crowd appeared.

Friday morning we were searching for a solution, when Joey suddenly said, "Police bullhorn."

Instantly I knew he was right. We jogged over to the city hall, and walked into Fuzzy Thurston's office. That's one of the great things about living in a town the size of Fairfield. Everybody knows everybody else. Fuzzy is our Chief of Police—in fact he's just about the whole Police Department. I've known Fuzzy since before I can remember. He plays pinochle with Pop, and teaches in our Sunday school.

"Hi, Fuzzy," I said.

"Hello, Chief," said Joey.

Fuzzy looked up from the papers he was signing. "Howdy, boys." He got up, walked around his desk, and shook hands with each of us.

Fuzzy treats everybody with respect. His hand is not much bigger than mine. Fuzzy is a skinny little guy, and you can't imagine him clobbering a vicious criminal, but everybody in Fairfield thinks he's the best chief of police in the state, and maybe the world.

"People tell me you boys are going to put on the world's biggest parade tomorrow. Did you get a parade permit?"

I looked at Joey. He swallowed hard. "We didn't know we needed one," I said.

"Boys, I'm joshing you." There was a twinkle in Fuzzy's eyes. "Adults need a permit for a parade through Fairfield, but I've just this minute written a new police regulation that kids under fourteen don't need a parade permit. Especially when they are raising money for Timmy Belasco's new kidney. Now, what can I do to help?"

"Bullhorn," said Joey.

"Well, I think that can be arranged. We bought a bullhorn ten years ago, in case we ever had to stand off a safe distance while we talked to a criminal, but we've never had that kind of situation." Fuzzy walked to a metal cabinet in the corner of his office. He reached into the cabinet, then placed a big bullhorn on his desk.

I'd never seen one except in the police programs on television. The bullhorn was shaped kind of like a bell with a handle on the bottom.

"Here's the on-off switch," said Fuzzy, pointing. "And this knob adjusts the volume." He handed the bullhorn to Joey.

Joey looked through Fuzzy's office window, which was open. Anne Lyon was window-shopping across Main Street. Joey pushed the on-off button, and the bullhorn crackled. He turned up the volume knob as far as it would go, lifted the bullhorn to his lips, and aimed it through the open window.

"Boo!" Joey said.

The bullhorn didn't just say "boo." It said, "BOOOOOO!!!"

Anne acted like she had been struck by a semitrailer truck on Interstate 80. She jumped at least two feet in the air, and when she came down she staggered backward and disappeared right through the door of McClennan's Department Store.

"Wow!" Joey whispered.

"WOOOOOWWWWW!!!" shouted the bullhorn.

★ ★ ★

We spent Friday afternoon at Joey's house making collection cans for the parade donations. We made them out of old tin cans wrapped with pink construction paper. On each one we lettered, with a felt-tip pen, "Timmy Belasco Kidney Transplant Fund."

It was a good way to get some of the other kids involved, especially the girls. I'd called Angela Hibbs and asked her to help. She showed up at Joey's house with three of her friends. As soon as she walked through the door, the soles of my feet started tingling. When she smiled at me—a special smile—I wondered if she was tingling, too. She turned up her nose at Sue Long, though, because Sue Long treats me like I'm her hero.

The girls brought tin cans and empty milk cartons. By the time they left, late in the afternoon, we had about a hundred collection cans ready to accept cash. I hoped we'd need them all.

I stopped tingling when Angela walked back out the door and headed home. Sue batted her eyes at me, and I started tingling again.

★   ★   ★

When I woke up Saturday morning, the first thing I heard was the rumble of thunder. Rain, driven by a heavy wind, sloshed against my bedroom window. I didn't want to face a stormy world on parade day, so I pulled the blanket up over my head. That gives a kid a wonderful feeling of security.

In about five minutes I wasn't breathing so good. I knew I had to face the world. All of a sudden I flung back the covers and leaped out of bed. When you *have* to do something you don't want to do, then do it so fast you don't have time to think about it. You might want to remember that tip; it could improve your life.

Little Timmy Belasco must be one of the world's greatest kids, despite his bad kidney. How else can you explain that the thunder muttered off into silence, and the skies suddenly cleared? It was an omen. This was going to be a good day. It was going to be a good parade. I could feel it in my bones as I headed into town on my bicycle.

Joey's eyes had a special shine when he opened the door. I left my bicycle at his house, and an hour before the parade was scheduled to start, we headed off toward the high school football field out on the edge of Fairfield. Joey was carrying the bullhorn.

We walked through the gate, around the bleachers, and onto the track that circles the football field. I couldn't believe my eyes. There must have been a hundred kids there already, milling around and goofing off like kids do when they have to wait. Millard Wiggins was beating Okey Doaks over the head with his baseball cap, and at the far end of the field three kids were dangling from the crossbar of the football goalpost.

About fifty more kids were horsing around up in the bleachers. They let out a cheer when they saw Joey and me walk onto the track with the bullhorn.

We climbed through the kids up to the top row of the bleachers. Joey turned on the bullhorn, and lifted it to his lips. He took a deep breath. There was a long pause. He turned and handed the bullhorn to me.

"Can't do it," he whispered.

"CAN'T DO IT!" shouted the bullhorn.

The kids around us jeered.

"Your attention, please," I said into the mouth-

piece. "ATTENTION PLEASE ATTENTION PLEASE!" my own voice echoed back from the far ends of the football field.

Millard Wiggins stopped hitting Okey. Gradually the kids quieted down.

"We've got to get this parade organized," I said. I learned right away to speak slowly because of the echo. "Joey and I want you to separate into three groups. Anybody who brought a musical instrument should go to the goalpost on my left." I waved my hand. "That's where the band will form up. Willie Duff will be the director and will tell you what to do." I paused. "All you girls who want to help collect money for Timmy Belasco's kidney should meet Angela Hibbs under the goalpost to my right." I waved my hand again. "Angela will give you a collection can and tell you what to do.

"Everybody left over who wants to be in the parade to help Timmy Belasco should meet in the middle of the football field. Okay, gang. Move!"

I looked down at the field. Kids started running everywhere, banging into each other, pushing and shoving. "This is not going to be easy," I said to Joey, being careful to turn off the bullhorn before I spoke. "This could turn into a real disaster."

Joey nodded. "But it's for Timmy."

Hundreds of other kids were pouring through the gates and onto the field, where they collided with the kids already there. It reminded me of a time when I threw a stick at a huge anthill. The ants were calmly going about their work before the stick hit. Right after that they were moving in a zillion different directions.

Beyond the main gate I could see a flashing blue light. Probably it was Fuzzy Thurston in the police car, checking to make sure everything was all right. It gave me kind of a warm feeling.

Joey and I managed to push across the field to the far goalpost. There were about two hundred kids waiting to be in the band. I'd never seen most of them before. Kids apparently were showing up from all over the state. They were carrying the strangest collection of musical instruments ever assembled. Already, I figured that we'd set a new record for the world's weirdest band.

There were some real instruments, of course. I spotted half a dozen trumpets, a couple of trombones, a flute, and a snare drum. Over on the edge of the field four high school girls were squawking away on violins. Todd Tinsley was there with his big string bass, and his little brother was there to help him carry it while he marched.

Most of the other kids were carrying things that would make a lot of noise, but you wouldn't exactly see them in the New York Philharmonic. Bill Barton was carrying a big galvanized bucket that he hit every now and then with a hickory branch. Dennis Taranowski had a four-foot length of garden hose with a funnel forced into one end; when he blew into the other end it sounded like an owl hooting during the full moon.

An older kid I remembered seeing at the TV station held two dented hubcaps that he beat together in rhythm. Velma Haag carried big metal salt and pepper shakers filled with tiny bells that she shook in time to the dented hubcaps; she did a little square-dance step at the end of every beat.

There were mouthharps and jawharps and willow whistles and turkey calls. There were real bass drums and homemade bass drums. There were dozens of kazoos, and everywhere we turned kids were humming into combs covered with tissue paper.

Best of all, I thought, was Punkin Farlow doing his head-bonking act. Punkin holds his mouth just so, then hits himself on the side of the head, and out of his mouth comes a loud *bonk*. The tone depends on how he holds his mouth. I've heard him do a spectacular "Stars and Stripes Forever."

Willie Duff had brought along a plumber's helper and an old packing crate. He placed the crate beneath the football goalpost, and climbed up on it. Then he blew on a whistle so hard he almost turned himself inside out. The kids became quiet. Kind of.

"Okay, let's practice!" Willie hollered. "How many of you know 'When the Saints Go Marching In'?"

Most of the kids raised their hands. One of them was Tom Boodle, who is the hottest trumpet player in Warren G. Harding School. Willie pointed at him. "Tom, you play one chorus of it," he shouted.

Tom put his gleaming trumpet to his lips. The notes that came out were pure gold. By the time he was halfway through, almost everybody in the stadium was quiet, listening.

"Thanks," shouted Willie. "Now let's all play it together." He raised the plumber's helper, pointing the handle toward the sky. Then he started pumping it up and down like a drum major.

I couldn't believe the racket. It *did* sound a little like saints marching somewhere or other. But if Tom Boodle had played one chorus in the key of F, then the other band members were playing in every other key previously known to man, and a good many new keys that had never been invented until that very moment.

Joey grabbed my arm. "Let's go!" he said. "I can't stand any more of this."

I sidled over to Willie Duff. Just as I started shouting up at him, the band came to the last note of the march. "*Sounds terrible!*" I hollered. My voice was the only sound at that end of the stadium. The whole band heard me, and started hollering back. I could tell they were having fun. "Willie, you have fifteen more minutes for band practice. Then we're starting the parade."

Willie nodded.

Joey and I pushed our way through the sea of kids. By now there were thousands on that football field. We broke up two fights on our way back to the bleachers. When we reached the top row, we found Dan Miner and Willy Peters sitting side by side.

"Hi, guys," I said. Joey nodded at the two men.

"Howdy, boys," said Dan. "You have quite a turnout. How can I help?"

"As the Grand Marshal—that means the honored guest—you'll lead the whole parade," I explained.

"Do you want me to drive my car?"

"No. We have a special vehicle for you. It's waiting on Oak Street just outside the gate to the stadium. The parade will start from there. As soon as I get these kids organized, we'll head over there."

Joey handed me the bullhorn. I switched it on, and turned the volume all the way up.

"*Attention!*" I shouted. "*Attention!*" At first the kids paid no heed, but the longer I shouted the quieter they got.

Finally I hollered, "We're going to start the parade in ten minutes at the Oak Street gate. Dan Miner will lead."

A wave of shouts and applause rolled over the stadium at the mention of his name. It showed how popular he was. Dan stood up and clasped his hands over his head like a boxer.

"Following Dan Miner will come the band, led by Willie Duff." This time a barrage of boos echoed across the field. I could see Willie's small figure standing on his box under the goalpost. He waved his plumber's helper.

"After that will come the rest of you, four abreast." Instantly, kids began grabbing other kids so they could march together.

"Most important of all," I said into the bullhorn, "don't forget that we are marching for a cause. An important cause. *Timmy Belasco!*" "Timmy Belasco, Timmy Belasco," the name echoed back from the stadium.

"Anything you can do, any little act you can perform, do it for Timmy. Turn cartwheels for Timmy. Make faces for Timmy."

Down on the playing field, kids began doing all kinds of outlandish things.

"A final note to you girls who are marching beside the parade to collect donations for the kidney fund. Smile your prettiest. Every dollar counts. Okay, gang. Let's march!"

With Joey in the lead, followed by Dan Miner, we pushed our way down the bleachers and across the field toward the Oak Street gate. The kids parted in front of us because of Dan Miner, who showed his teeth and reached out to shake hands like he was running for office.

The Aldrich twins were waiting for us at the gate with the Grand Marshal's carriage. Dan Miner and Willy Peters started laughing when they saw it.

We'd given Brady and Grady the job of coming up with something spectacular to lead the parade. They'd developed a strange three-in-one unit. Grady was riding the Aldrich family mower, and Brady was seated on another power mower he had borrowed. The mowers, in turn, were connected by ropes to a little trailer that Noah Oostermeyer uses to haul manure around his farm. The twins had pretty well cleaned up the trailer. Pretty well.

An easy chair, borrowed from Stanton's Furniture Close-Outs, had been set up in the bed of the trailer like a throne. A banner along the side of the trailer said, "Our Grand Marshal, Dan Miner." The girls had decorated the trailer with crepe-paper streamers and balloons.

It was a colorful sight. Dan Miner had a big grin on his face when he put his foot atop one of the tires and swung himself up into the trailer and onto the throne. But I noticed he quickly covered his grin with his handkerchief, which he held up to his nose.

Grady and Brady revved up their mowers. The rope stretched, and the trailer eased forward.

The World's Largest Kids' Parade was under way!

★   ★   ★

I'll bet you're already thinking that all those zillions of kids turned into a disorganized mob. Well, you're wrong. If you give kids a *reason* to do something good—or bad—then they'll nearly always do it. That's a good thought for the day. We'd given them a reason to do something good.

First, of course, came Grady and Brady Aldrich on their mowers. Then came Dan Miner proudly sitting atop his throne. Joey and I sniffled along behind Noah Oostermeyer's manure trailer, followed by Willie Duff waving his big baton and blowing his whistle every time we turned a corner.

There were more than two hundred kids in the band alone. They marched down the street ten abreast. As we turned onto Highland Avenue, Willie blew his whistle three times, raised his baton high above his head, then dropped it to his waist. The band crashed into "When the Saints Go Marching In."

It was absolutely awful. At least for the first half-mile. They all played in a different key. Some played fast, some slow. Some played soft, but most played loud. Some finished the song a full block ahead of others.

I glanced at Joey; he had his hands over his ears. Ahead of us, Dan Miner's face popped up over the back of his throne. There was a big question mark on his face. I tried to smile as I waved at him.

Then a funny thing happened. By the time the band played halfway through the piece again, most of them were playing in the same key. Actually, it sounded pretty good. And instead of staggering along, the kids were keeping step. They were playing music, and they were marching!

I turned around and walked backward so I could watch them. Willie Duff's proud grin was as wide as his face. He'd created a mammoth marching band!

Just behind Willie marched Angela's little sister Samantha, who had taken baton-twirling lessons in Center City for six months. She was almost as pretty as Angela. While I was watching she twirled the baton so fast you could hardly see it, then threw it high in the air. It wasn't such a hot throw because it arched sideways and came down in Mrs. Smithers's prize rose garden. I ran over to the curb, and pushed through a big batch of people who were watching the parade. I jumped across the fence and landed in the middle of Mrs. Smithers's roses. When I found the baton, I turned to rejoin the parade and bopped into Mrs. Smithers's purple dress. She wears it everywhere. I got out of there in a hurry. It just shows how you can get into trouble trying to do a good turn for someone else.

Back in the parade, I handed the baton to Samantha and tried to make her understand, over the noise of the band, that she didn't have to throw it so high to impress the spectators.

Talk about spectators! Willy Peters's publicity campaign had really paid off. As we marched through the outskirts of town, people came running out of their houses, waving and shouting.

My pride took a nosedive, though, when we turned the corner and swung up Elm Street. We were still out on the edge of town at that point. Stretch Wolters owns a big field adjoining the city limits, where he used to pasture his cows before he sold them all a year ago. Now there was a big sign at the gate to the pasture that read:

PARKING FOR THE
TIMMY BELASCO KIDNEY FUND PARADE
Courtesy Willy Peters Enterprises
$2.50 per car

I couldn't believe my eyes. Drivers from every town in our part of the state actually were begging to pay good money to drive onto the field. Willy's cousin Jasper was stuffing the money into his overall pockets as fast as his hands could move.

Now I knew how Willy was going to make his money off our parade. Made me madder than a horse-fly without a horse. I guess I shouldn't have been mad at Willy, though. He'd earned anything he'd take in.

Finally we turned off Elm Street and headed up Main Street through Fairfield's business district. People were lined up along the curb seven or eight deep.

Up ahead I could see the blue light flashing on top of Fuzzy's police car. It was parked right in front of city hall. Fuzzy was trying to push people back so the Aldrich twins could ride through on their mowers, towing Dan Miner.

There were a lot more people gathered around the city square than actually *lived* in Fairfield. I wondered why; then I knew. Dan Miner and Willy Peters had attracted hundreds and hundreds of kids to Fairfield from towns as far away as Center City—and *those kids had been brought there by their parents.* I'll bet there also were a lot of grandparents, aunts, uncles, and cousins in the crowd.

I held out my hands, palm up, to Joey. After all, the whole thing had been his idea. He slapped my hands. We dropped out to watch our creation from the steps of city hall.

The band blasted past. Horns tooted. Drums and galvanized buckets beat out the cadence. A pair of cymbals clanged. Actually the cymbals were two garbage-can lids in the hands of Spud Hornfeld, who is the biggest kid at Garfield School.

Everybody was clapping and yahooing. Samantha heaved her baton again. I held my breath as the baton made a silvery arc across the sky. It must have gone much higher than Samantha had ever thrown it before. As soon as it left her hands, she started running. She darted through the crowd, ran right up over a park bench, landed on the other side, reached out as far as she could, lost her balance, and rolled over twice. When she got to her feet her face was triumphant. In her hand she held the baton. The crowd loved it.

After the band passed by, Joey and I watched the

other kids put on their own performances. A boy I'd never seen before rolled past on a unicycle. Five girls tap-danced along wearing short skirts and sweaters that said "Center City School of the Performing Arts."

Pat Tooley marched sedately along reciting the capital cities of all the states in alphabetical order. Two strange kids walked past on their hands, their faces red as ripe apples. Ward Huxley strolled by pulling his little brother in a homemade rickshaw. Patty Bean danced along with her two pet garter snakes draped around her neck.

Standing on the steps of city hall, I heard adult voices behind me. I turned around. Three different TV crews had set up their equipment. They were all from different channels, and two were from the networks.

"Big-time stuff," I said to Joey.

By now we could spot some of our girl collectors making their way along the parade route, trying to look beautiful while they shook their collection boxes and cans in people's faces. And people were responding. I watched Melissa Hinks smile at an old man with a white beard. He dropped a dollar bill into her coffee can. She shook the can again, blew him a kiss, and he dropped in a five-dollar bill.

Betts was watching the parade from the doorway of McClennan's Department Store, where she works. She didn't really look like my good old sister Betts because her stomach was sticking way out in front of her. But when she smiled and waved at me, it was just like old times, like nothing had come between us. I waved back.

Sue Long, her blond ponytail swinging this way and that, had collected so much money that her coffee can was overflowing. She ran over and dumped the contents into Dan Miner's lap, then ran along the parade route collecting more.

I checked my watch. By now the parade had been going on for almost an hour. The last of the kids were straggling past, big gaps between them. Spectators began to turn away. But when a shout went up, they turned back.

Joey grabbed my shoulder. He pointed. "Look!"

My eyes turned up Main Street.

Pop came striding down the street on his fifteen-foot stilts, waving right and left to the people down below. He just couldn't resist the World's Biggest Parade. I had to give him credit. After his disastrous run on the stilts I didn't think he'd ever try them again. He told me later he'd talked Noah Oostermeyer and his hired man into helping him up on his stilts. And here he was, weaving back and forth across Main Street, basking in the applause of the crowd.

"Well, that's the end of the parade," I said to Joey as Pop moved on up the street.

"Turn it around," said Joey.

"Turn what around?"

"Turn the parade around. I want to see the whole thing again."

★ ★ ★

The girls had been asked to bring their collection cans to Joey's house after the parade. We poured all the money out on the Gootz's living room carpet.

We found everything from pennies to a fifty-dollar bill. Before we were through we had a stack of signed checks six inches high; three Canadian quarters; a token for a ride on the Ferris wheel in Center City; and a coupon for a free sample box of Toasty-Oh cereal.

It took Joey and me two hours just to get the money organized into stacks. Then we counted it. Each of us, separately. We were off by $637.81. By then it was getting dark and we were beginning to fight over who was the best counter, so I headed home.

The next morning I showed up early, and we started counting all over again. This time we were $821.67 off. So we tried once more.

On Monday, Dan Miner called. "Pete," he said, "can you and Joey appear on 'Stars of Tomorrow' this week, and tell everybody how much you collected for the Timmy Belasco Kidney Fund?"

"Sure. We don't know how much we have yet, but we'll know by Saturday morning."

Later in the week, Willy Peters volunteered to run us over to the studio. I was mad at him for making money on the parking lot, but Joey pointed out how much Willy had contributed to the success of the parade. So on Saturday we let Willy drive us to the TV studio.

Joey and I sat on one side of Dan Miner, and Willy sat on the other. When the light signaled that we were on the air, Dan bonged his gong, and then raised his arms in a "V," like he always does. The kids in the studio went crazy.

Dan smiled his big smile and said, "Dan Miner proudly presents three stars of tomorrow, three young men who planned and produced the Timmy Belasco Kidney Fund Parade, now famous throughout the world. Peter Potts! Joey Gootz! Willy Peters!"

There was a recorded fanfare from a dozen trumpets, and the kids hollered again.

I didn't like the way Dan was including Willy Peters on the program. Willy sat there grinning and nodding, like he was responsible for the whole thing.

"And now for the important part of the program," said Dan. "Boys, how much money did the parade raise for Timmy Belasco's kidney transplant?"

"$15,613.96," I said.

"$16,241.84," said Joey.

Dan Miner laughed. "Well, no matter what it is, it's a mighty big contribution, and for a mighty worthy cause."

Willy waved his arms. "No. There's more than that," he said.

I was already riled at Willy, and this made me madder than a wet rooster. "How do you know?" I said. "You didn't even count it."

"I mean," said Willy, "that there's still more money to be included in the kidney fund." Willy was speaking very slowly, as though it was difficult for him to spit out the words.

"What money?" I asked.

"The money from the parking lot." He pulled a piece of paper from his pocket and looked at it. "$3,894.67."

Suddenly I liked Willy better than I ever had before. I knew how difficult this was for him. Willy doesn't give away money, he takes it. I did something that kids don't very often do. I reached across and shook hands with Willy. Joey did the same.

"That makes a grand total of something over $20,000," said Dan Miner into his microphone. "That won't pay for Timmy's operation, but it certainly has started the ball rolling. Contributions are pouring in to the studio from all over the state. And Timmy's doctor tells me that all the publicity may help locate a kidney donor, which is what Timmy is waiting for now."

Loud applause.

"And now for the big surprise!" Dan Miner looked expectantly off to the right.

There was a scuffling sound from that direction. Two men dressed in white uniforms appeared, pushing a stretcher along on wheels. There was a little pile of blankets in the middle of the stretcher. Joey and I stood up to get a better look.

Timmy Belasco was obviously in pain, but when he saw us his face lit up like a spotlight. "Hi, Joey!" he said in a weak but happy voice. "Hi, Pete!"

"Hi, Timmy." Joey's voice was soft. There was a special smile on his face. "Gonna get you a new kidney, Kiddo."

THE WORLD'S BIGGEST KID PARADE.

The parade occurred on Saturday, July 19, and marched through the streets of Fairfield. An estimated 1,350 kids paraded a distance of 3 1/2 miles without a single fistfight, as far as is known. The parade was conceived and organized by Joey Gootz, Peter Potts, and Willy Peters. It resulted in a new kidney. I witnessed the event and hereby swear it is a new world's record.

Peter Potts

☆ 5 ☆

The World's Best

I know all about women having babies. At least *almost* all about it. As much as I *want* to know about it.

I know women get bigger and bigger. I thought Maybelle Seymour was going to fall over on her face before she finally had her baby.

But Betts had always been neat and trim. It didn't seem like she *ever* should get fat. Then, back on the very first day of summer vacation, I glanced out the window and saw her stooping over in her rose garden. She stood up and stretched. Her middle looked thick; she didn't have much of a waist.

That same week she quit the Maid-Rite Maids Industrial Softball Team, which is a shame because she can hit a softball half a mile, and flip a grounder to first base so fast you'd swear you heard it sizzle.

She not only quit playing softball, but when she got even bigger she quit her job at McClennan's Department Store. She said Mike insisted that she stop working.

Betts kept getting bigger and bigger all summer. Criminy, did she get big!

I know it takes nine months to make a baby, but those months dragged on and on. Seems like they should be able to shorten the process.

On the other hand, I didn't *want* the baby to come.

One night, while I was setting the table for supper, she said, "Only one month to go, Pete." She was stirring the stew; by now her stomach was so far out in front that she could barely reach the stove.

"Only one month to go until what?" I asked. I was thinking in terms of school starting.

"Pete, you're a lovable nitwit," she said. "You know what I mean. Only one month to go until the baby comes."

"Too bad!" I said. I slammed the last plate down on the table and walked out of the kitchen.

There were tears in Betts's eyes during supper. I was truly sorry for what I'd said.

★ ★ ★

About a week later I woke up to the drumming of rain on the roof. Maybe you can remember how dark it gets during a late August thunderstorm. It was so dark that we had to turn on the lights during breakfast.

Pop and Mike went off to work wearing raincoats

and old shoes. Thunder rumbled and echoed across the sky.

I dialed Joey's number. "C'mon over," I said.

"What for?"

"I dunno what for. But at least we can do what-for together."

Joey was agreeable. There hadn't been any excitement in our lives since the Timmy Belasco parade. We hadn't even tried to set any more world's records.

Fifteen minutes later Joey arrived, trailing a little river of water across the floor. Betts didn't seem to care. Lightning flashed through the open windows, and the weeping willow branches brushed against the kitchen wall in sudden gusts of wind.

Betts started cleaning the stove. She always makes a big production out of that job, scouring all the burners and scrubbing every corner of the oven. She says you can't produce good food on a dirty stove. That's a big thought, and one that means a lot more than it seems to say.

There didn't seem to be much else to do, so I got out the Monopoly game. Joey helped me spread everything out on the kitchen table. We each rolled the dice to see who'd be the banker. I won, and counted out the money. I shortchanged Joey, but I swear I didn't do it on purpose. He gouged me in the chest with his elbow.

Things got pretty hot in that game right away. Joey locked onto three of the four railroads, and both the electric company and the water works. I was having bad luck with the dice, and every time I went around the board I landed on one of his railroads. Cost me a fortune.

In Monopoly, I've always had good luck with the yellow deeds. I concentrated on that. I got the deeds to Atlantic Avenue and Marvin Gardens.

Things were looking good until Joey landed on Ventnor Avenue. A big smile crossed his face. He knew how much I wanted that yellow deed to make my set complete. And I knew there was no way I could get it.

Then, by an incredible stroke of luck, I landed on the fourth railroad. I shouted, "I'll buy it!"

Now each of us had a deed the other desperately wanted.

"Let's swap," I said.

"No. You give me a thousand dollars and it's a deal." Joey has always been pretty sharp at Monopoly; he was waving the deed to Ventnor Avenue right in front of my eyes.

"Five hundred dollars," I said. My voice was weak. I wanted that yellow deed so bad I was tempted to pay the thousand.

There was a moan from the direction of the stove. "Better do it!" Betts's voice was strangely shrill.

"Naw," said Joey. "I'm holding out for a thousand."

"No," she said. "Not Monopoly. You'd better do

it, Pete. You'd better call the ambulance right away.
And call Dr. Shuck, too!"

I turned around and looked at her. She was leaning
against the stove. Her face was white. Sweat ran down
her forehead.

I got slowly to my feet. "What's wrong?"

"The baby's coming."

"It can't be!" I protested. "It isn't time yet."

Betts pressed both hands against her stomach. "I'm
having labor pains." She spoke through clenched teeth.
"The baby's coming, Pete. I've got to get to the hospital."

"But that's all the way over in Center City," I said.
We didn't have a hospital in Fairfield. Not yet. The
Lion's Club is raising money for one.

"Pete, I've got to get to the hospital right away!"
A pain spasm crossed her face. She walked over and
eased herself down onto the chair I'd vacated. Then
she moaned, and grabbed my stack of hundred-dollar
bills. Her knuckles were white. I had the crazy thought
that we'd never get all the wrinkles out of that money.

"What'll we do?" asked Joey.

"I'm afraid to move very much until the ambulance
arrives. I'll just sit here. Pete, call the ambulance right
now. Ron Sievers probably will be on duty. Tell him
to get here as fast as he can."

Betts and Ron had gone through school together.
He'd always wanted to be a doctor, but when his dad
died he'd given up college and trained to be a medic.

I knew he'd take special care of Betts as soon as he arrived.

"After you've called the ambulance, call Dr. Shuck and tell him I'm on my way to the hospital. I'm sure he'll get there as fast as he can. Then call Mike and tell him—" Another spasm of pain moved across her face. She moaned.

"What can I do to help?" asked Joey.

She managed a little smile. As I turned and headed for the phone in the living room, I heard her say, "Joey, get the suitcase from my closet. Pack it with anything you think I might need in the hospital."

My fingers were shaking as I dialed the emergency number for the ambulance.

"County Emergency Service," a voice crackled in my ear.

"That you, Ron?" I asked.

"Sure is. Who's on the other end?"

"Pete. Peter Potts."

"What's up, Pete?"

"Betts's baby is coming. We've got to get her to the hospital right away."

"Keep calm, Pete. Tell Betts I'll be right there." The line went dead.

I hung up and dialed Doc Shuck. His number was taped right next to the phone. His nurse answered.

"I've got to talk to the doctor right away. Emergency." I tried to make my voice sound official, but it was shrill.

"The doctor is out. I expect him back in ten or fifteen minutes. Is there anything I can do?"

"This is Peter Potts. Tell Dr. Shuck that my sister Betts is going to have her baby. Now. Anyway soon. And she's on her way by ambulance to Center City. She wants the doctor to meet her at the hospital."

"I'll tell him as soon as I can, Peter. Maybe I can reach him by phone. Tell Betts to keep calm, and he'll see her at the hospital."

I ran back to the kitchen. Betts was groaning. Her face glistened with sweat. "I think you'd better help me into bed, Pete." She spoke each word with great effort.

Joey trotted into the kitchen, opened a cupboard door, took down a jar of peanut butter, and trotted out again.

I helped Betts up from the table. Once she was on her feet she seemed to improve. She sighed and straightened her dress. "Pain's gone. That's better. But I think I'd better lie down until the ambulance comes."

I helped her to her bedroom just behind the kitchen, and eased her down onto the bed. She was moaning again.

By now, Joey was over in one corner of the bedroom squatting beside her suitcase, which was on the floor. He glanced at me. I could see a worried look on his face. The suitcase was open. Inside was a jumble of underwear, jeans, socks, cheese crackers, peanut butter, and taco shells. He tossed her rubber boots on top, and sat on the suitcase in an effort to close it.

Betts's breath was coming in gasps. "Call Mike right away, Pete. Tell him to get here as soon as he can. If I'm not here, I'm on the way to the hospital. Tell him to call Pop." She panted out the words.

I ran back to the phone. The girl in Mike's office said that he'd stepped out for coffee, but she'd run over to the Kozy Kup and give him the message. Fine time for him to be drinking coffee, I thought. Why wasn't he home at a time like this?

I started toward the bedroom. The phone rang, so I ran back to answer it. "Hello!" I shouted. "I'm having a baby! Get off the phone!"

"Calm down, Pete! This is Ron Sievers."

I exploded. "Doggone it, you're supposed to be on your way over here!"

"Pete, listen carefully. We can't get the ambulance started."

"You WHAT!"

"I think it's the carburetor."

"I DON'T CARE WHAT IT IS, YOU GET OVER HERE RIGHT AWAY!"

Just then there was a shriek from Betts's bedroom. I tried to fight down the panic. "Betts is shouting. I've got to go check on her. I'll be right back."

I left the phone dangling and ran for the bedroom. Her eyes were closed, but she was moaning and gritting her teeth. I didn't have the heart to tell her about the carburetor. She heard me when I ran in, and opened her eyes.

"The baby's coming! Soon! I can tell!"

Joey, sitting on the suitcase, had eyes as big as his face.

"I'll be right back!" I patted her on the shoulder. "Got something to do."

Back at the phone, I said, as clearly and distinctly as I could, "Betts says the baby is coming. Right away. What should I do?"

There was a long pause. Then, "Listen to me, Pete. Get all the towels you can find. Also, boil a bucket of water. Sam Perkins and I are on our way in my car."

"But—"

"Keep your head, Pete! You've got to stay calm. I've already located Doc Shuck. Now go get those towels, and have the hot water ready when we arrive."

I hung up, and took time for a deep breath. Doggone that baby. Someday I'd get even. I ran to Betts's room.

She was calm, and her eyes were open. "It's going to be all right, big fellow," she said softly. She hadn't called me that since I was five or six years old.

"Sure. I know." I looked down. I knew I couldn't lie to her. "Betts, there's something I've got to tell you. Ron can't get the ambulance started. He and Sam Perkins are on their way over here in a car."

"EEEEEEEEE—" There was a kind of a moan from

the corner, like the sound of a pine tree in a windstorm. I glanced over at Joey. He sat there on the suitcase with his hands over his ears and his eyes closed.

"It's okay," Betts said calmly. "I've known for several minutes that the baby will be born here. Born right in his own home. And you'll help me, Pete." There was the same trust in her eyes as the time I helped her scare the snake away from the wren's nest. Suddenly she moaned. Her body convulsed. When the pain passed, she said, "Help me get my clothes off, and throw a sheet over me."

I took command. "Joey, get all the towels out of the linen closet and bring them here." I was surprised at the authority in my voice. "After you've done that, fill a big pan with water and put it on the stove." He sat there with his hands over his ears. "*Get moving!*" I shouted.

Joey skedaddled out of the room.

I tried to get Betts out of her clothes, but she couldn't seem to move her body to help me. She was in constant pain. Finally I got a pair of scissors and cut her underwear from her. I couldn't help but notice the rolling motion inside her stomach.

"Pull a sheet—" she started to say, then let out the biggest moan of all. When she regained control she said in a low voice, "Pull a sheet over me. Keep it loose at the bottom of the bed."

I pulled the sheet over her. Joey came through the door balancing a huge stack of towels. He stumbled over one of Betts's shoes, and the towels ended up all over Betts. Only once have I ever seen Joey look as horror-stricken as he did at that moment, and that's when he saw the Great Creeping Slime from the movie of the same name. He managed to stumble through the door into the kitchen.

"Hold my hand, big fellow." I couldn't believe the softness in Betts's voice. I took her hand between mine, and squeezed. She squeezed back. Suddenly she began squeezing in a definite rhythm. You didn't have to be a doctor to know it was the rhythm of a baby being born.

Joey stuck his head through the doorway. "Is this one okay?" He was holding Grandma's soup kettle.

Suddenly I felt woozy. It was all I could do to nod at Joey. Slowly the room began to spin. I knew I was going to faint. I'd fainted once before, when I watched them make pickles at the packing plant.

Betts screamed, and at the same moment she squeezed my hand like she wanted to break the bones. The room was spinning faster. I thought I heard the crunch of gravel in the driveway. I imagined that I heard the scream of a siren in the distance. Or was it Betts screaming again?

The screen door banged twice, and two or three different voices were hollering in the living room.

I found myself on my knees beside the bed. I closed my eyes. I *had* to help Betts. She was counting on me.

"Waaaaaaaaaaaaaa—" It was the faint cry of a baby. I opened my eyes. There it was. The baby, I mean.

Only inches from my face. It had two tiny legs, and two arms, and all four of them were jerking. There was blood on the baby. I should clean it up.

My head began to clear. I grabbed a towel, and somehow rolled the baby over on it. Something still connected the baby to Betts. I got to my feet just as the door banged open. Suddenly the room was full of people. Mike was smiling down at Betts with love and worry in his eyes, and she was smiling back. Ron Sievers and Sam Perkins were there, carrying a stretcher. Over in the corner Pop was having a conniption doing what I figured must be a great-grandfatherly jig.

Doc Shuck came through the doorway, a medical bag in his hand, followed by Fuzzy Thurston.

The baby yelped again, and squirmed in my arms. There was sudden quiet in the room, as though somebody had given a signal. As a matter of fact, my baby *had* given a signal.

It seemed like that quiet stretched out halfway to Mexico. Everyone stood like statues, looking down at the baby in my arms.

Finally I said, "Look what I've got."

There was a warm bubble in the middle of my stomach. Like a bubble of pride.

We were a *family*, and we had a brand-new member so small I couldn't believe it was alive. It was beautiful in spite of being so red and scrawny.

Mike stepped over and reached out his arms. "My baby," he said, in a voice like he was living on Mars.

"*Our* baby," I said. But I handed it to him.

He took the baby in his arms. He cradled it for a moment, then placed it on the bed beside Betts. He kissed Betts on the forehead. Mushy.

Doc Shuck bustled forward. "As soon as I cut the cord and check you over," he said to Betts, "we'll rush you to the hospital."

"Boy?" asked Betts weakly.

"Girl," said Doc Shuck. "A fine little girl."

Ron and Sam started unfolding the stretcher.

I stood there without much to do. Then the baby hollered at me. I could tell she was hollering at me because she waved her tiny little arms in my direction.

Joey came through the doorway lugging a soup kettle full of cold water. He was the one who broke the silence. "I can't figure out how to work your stove," he said, looking across at me.

"Look what we did," I said, motioning toward the baby.

"Wow!" he said. "WOW! What's its name?"

Dumb. Maybe he thought babies arrive in this world already equipped with names. Then I had an inspiration. It happened because a mental picture of Angela Hibbs and Sue Long flashed through my mind. Both of them at once. How pleased they'd be! "Angela," I said. "Angela Sue is the baby's name." They'd like me forever!

Betts repeated the name. "Angela Sue." She smiled.

As soon as she smiled, Mike said, "Sounds great to me."

Joey handed me the kettle of water. He stepped over and picked up some hundred-dollar Monopoly bills that were scattered across the bed. He stuffed them in his shirt pocket. "You're going to need these. Soon as everybody clears out, I'm going to sell you the deed to Ventnor Avenue for one thousand dollars."

"Five hundred," I said. "But the game will have to wait. I'm going to the hospital with our baby."

I looked down at Betts. A big tear rolled down her cheek and soaked into the pillow. "With *our* baby," she repeated as she smiled up at me.

THE WORLD'S GREATEST BABY.

She was born August 25 in her mother's bedroom at the Potts residence in Fairfield. Supervising the birth was Peter Potts, Uncle. Assistance was provided from the kitchen nearby by Joey Gootz. The baby was named Angela Sue Summers. She was rushed to the hospital in Center City, where the admitting doctor stated that the delivery had been executed flawlessly. If you doubt that she is the World's Greatest Baby, stop by and see her. I, the undersigned, will show her off to one and all.

Peter Potts,
Uncle